7/12

DISCARD

D1595853

FACE VALUE

Just released from prison for petty crime, Charlie has plans for a stainless but ambitious future. Employed as gardener-chauffeur to elderly Emily Penneston-Barkley, he endeavours to make himself indispensable with hopes of inheriting her lovely house. All seems happy until the girl whom the old lady believes is her niece Paula, from New York, pays a long overdue visit. Soon after arrival, the girl receives a telephone call from James Maddison in New York, with shocking news. James arrives in England with greedy designs on the house and inheritance. For this he is prepared to kill . . .

Books by Peggy Graham
Published by The House of Ulverscroft:

STONE WALLS
SCARLET ANGEL
WITCH OF THE WOOD

PEGGY GRAHAM

FACE VALUE

Complete and Unabridged

ULVERSCROFT
Leicester

First published in Great Britain in 2004

First Large Print Edition
published 2004

The moral right of the author has been asserted

British Library CIP Data

Graham, Peggy
    Face value.—Large print ed.—
    Ulverscroft large print series: crime
    1. Detective and mystery stories
    2. Large type books
    I. Title
    823.9'14 [F]

    ISBN 1–84395–147–9

Published by
F. A. Thorpe (Publishing)
Anstey, Leicestershire
Set by Words & Graphics Ltd.
Anstey, Leicestershire
Printed and bound in Great Britain by
T. J. International Ltd., Padstow, Cornwall

This book is printed on acid-free paper

Dedicated to my daughters and my husband
and to the precious memories of our
Priceless Treasure, Stuart John,
who will live in our hearts forever.

1956

1

The heavy door of the prison closed behind him with a loud thud and he stepped through to a welcoming breeze of liberty. The warm sunlight of early spring greeted him and he lifted his face to savour its soft kiss of freedom.

He paused briefly to take a deep ecstatic breath, then exhaled six months of incarceration from his life. From a pocket in his Harris tweed jacket he took an empty pipe, made of the best briarwood, and placed it between his teeth. Instantly his old self-confidence returned. Present lack of St Bruno did not bother him, he was not addicted. Quite simply the pipe complimented the natural air of sophistication that his refined looks projected.

Unhurried he let these first moments of regaining control of his life wash over him before moving on.

In the street two women glanced his way and quickly turned to look again. Fragments of their words drifted back to him . . . 'Visiting actor, sometimes play readings . . . ' He was familiar with this kind of status

3

assessment, always far from the real truth. People attached various mental labels to his appearance. In his Harris tweeds, of which he was extremely fond, he looked every inch a country squire; but because of his exceptional good looks actor was the most common.

He preferred the country-squire tag. In his opinion actors lived in a make-believe world and had no real class; and class was what he hankered for most of all.

The true-life status of Charlie Barnes was never correctly estimated by anyone other than those amongst whom he lived in one of the shabby back-streets of Dockland. At one end of Dock Street stood a pub on each corner, in one or the other of which his Ma could usually be found sipping at a glass of stout.

Not that Charlie blamed her too much for seeking escape for a while from the cramped confines of the two-up two-down terrace house that opened straight onto the street.

This was the lowly-born tag that Charlie's appearance belied. His education had been cut as short as was legally permissible. At the age of fourteen he had left school and started to work for his living. His Ma and Pa had been more concerned with their present than with his future. In fairness he had to admit that he had not been much of a scholar.

However hard he had tried it had been impossible for him to keep his mind on any school subject long enough to derive much academic benefit.

Until the age of sixteen he had taken a series of menial jobs, although none manual; labouring or navvying was not included on his employment menu. He despised the lot of the uneducated working classes.

It was at this stage that he'd first become aware of the attention he drew from females of all ages. He had not set out to do this. It just happened and to an extent that he could not help noticing.

At sixteen he had taken up employment as a hotel waiter. From there he had progressed to larger and better ones, each more star-worthy than the last.

In the last hotel he had made a close study of the wealthier guests, noting their speech, manners and general behaviour. That one he had considered as his finishing school.

Charlie took a short-cut across the park. As he walked he mused on his recent spell in prison. His one and only mad and stupid lapse from the straight and narrow. Besides himself there had been a few others in for burglary. All bragged that next time they wouldn't get caught. There would be no next time for Charlie Barnes. Inside he'd had plenty of time to take stock of his life . . . of himself. He decided that he needed direction in his life. Most of all he was determined to rise in the social world; to leave Dock Street behind him once and for all.

During those long days and nights inside he'd done a lot of thinking and planning and had come to a few conclusions. Brains secured positions denied to those without them. Well . . . perhaps he didn't have the brains, academically speaking, who could tell without an education? But looks could do as much. If you had looks you had power. He'd been told often enough that he had looks. The rest was just a matter of confidence. Anyone could put on an act. He'd already found it easy enough.

Humorous recollections tilted the corners of his mouth. He brought to mind the time when Tyler, a fellow waiter, had invited him to a high society party where, just for a lark, he had introduced him as an Italian Count.

Tyler was from an upper class society and had left home to make his own way in the world after a dispute with his father who was a prominent government minister.

The party had been given by friends from his own social class so it was thought no big deal that a count, Italian or otherwise, should be amongst the guests.

Charlie had risen to the challenge and played along. A hidden talent had surfaced. With ease he had discovered that he could manage a fair imitation of an Italian accent, along with some of that language picked up from hotel guests.

He had been popular with the girls at the party and had turned down invitations from two to visit their country homes. He would have liked to but he'd have been obliged to keep up that phoney accent. Anyway how could he think of becoming involved with a girl; sooner or later he would have to disclose his background. He couldn't keep his Ma a secret indefinitely. Often he'd tried to persuade her to move to a better district. But rented houses were still hard to come by. Adamantly she had scorned the idea. 'I like it well enough where I am. I don't want no posh 'ouse. A fine mess I'd be in when you left 'ome to get married and I couldn't afford to keep up the 'igh rent.'

Besides, even if he had been able to talk her into moving he couldn't cover up the way she spoke. She could never really mix outside of Dockland. He winced slightly now as he recalled an incidence from the past. One lunchtime when he'd been strolling through the town park with the receptionist from the hotel he had heard the vociferous voice of his

Ma calling across the grass to him . . . 'Yoo-hoo Chawl. I'll be out when you gets 'ome. I'll be in Mrs 'arris's if you wants me.'

He recalled the surprised expression on the face of the girl although she'd tried to hide it. Afterwards he had taxed his Ma about it. 'Showing me up like that ma!'

She had looked affronted for a moment then had answered. 'Aw — get away with yuh. I can't put me talk on like you — nor I don't want to neither.'

'And why do you always have to go about with those two things stuck in front of your hair?' He'd pointed to the two metal curlers embedded securely in the front of her hair above her forehead. Only at Sunday teatimes were they ever removed for a few hours.

Her hand had shot up to touch the offending rolls as if by some witchcraft they had been planted there without her consent or knowledge. Then in an affronted tone she had shouted, 'If your ashamed o' me I'll walk straight past ya' next time!'

At the time Charlie sincerely hoped that she meant it.

Then it was her turn to be ashamed. Secretly she'd been so proud of him. Everyone remarked on his good looks. They all knew that he'd been caught and convicted. During the time in which he'd committed the

8

offence he had been living away from home in cheap lodgings. But nevertheless the police had wanted to search the house in Dock Street.

Two young mothers seated on a park bench near the fish-pond watched Charlie as he passed. Still deep in reflection he did not notice them. He was remembering how his brief fall from grace had come about.

One evening a guest in the hotel where he worked at that time had struck up a conversation with him. The chap had been an area manager for encyclopaedias. He had claimed to earn what seemed a small fortune to Charlie who had been impressed and interested to hear more about the job.

So Charlie had given up the hotel job to sell, or try to sell, encyclopaedias.

This was not as easy as he had been led to believe. He did get to see the interiors of some decent class properties that fired his ambition to succeed himself. He could not imagine any of those people living in the rabbit hutches of Dock Street.

They all treated him with respectful interest and hospitality and always pressed him to stay a while chatting, although never about the encyclopaedias. Very few, if any, ever wanted to buy the books. Charlie had charm but no real sales ability. Either that or people just do not want to own encyclopaedias.

Then, by chance, in one house he recognised the occupant as previously being a Dockland dweller. He seemed fairly comfortably off and confided in Charlie about how he had achieved it all. He told him that he would never accomplish much from door to door sales and invited him on what he termed as 'a warehouse job'. That had been Charlie's undoing. By sheer bad luck he had been caught red-handed when the manager had for some reason returned to the premises late evening. Charlie could have fought him off, but he abhorred violence, and so surrendered quietly. The chap who had done the planning had managed to escape.

A ball came hurtling across his path and brought his thoughts back to the present. He stopped to kick it back towards a group of young boys farther over in the park and he heard one of them call . . . 'Thanks mister.'

Charlie crossed the grass to a flowerbed and paused to make a brief study of the plants. He could name each species; something that he could not have done before his short spell inside. This acquired knowledge was, he hoped, going to direct his immediate future. It was part of the plans that he had made during those incarcerated hours. He had come to this decision after considering other possibilities open to him. One less appealing, which he finally decided against, was to become a lounge-lizard. While working in the better hotels he had observed these types going about their business and been secretly amused and impressed by their tactics. The best hotel lounges were their operating ground. Impeccably dressed and trading on their face value they would sit around casting speculative eyes on unescorted female guests. Older women were the target, and vulnerable. No feminine woman was immune to a little flattery and polite attention from a presentable young gentleman. Invariably they responded, quite eagerly at times, to little deferential and chivalrous acts of courtesy.

Watching the smooth manoeuvres and skilful contrivances of these masters at their trade Charlie had been amazed at the ease with which they accomplished their aims. If they judged well some would with a little luck live on easy-street, perhaps in luxury with their elderly conquests. Some, he'd been told, went as far as marriage and eventually came into small fortunes.

Being bilingual gave a wider field in which to operate. He had watched one chap approach an elegantly dressed older French woman. Being able to converse in her native tongue had given him a distinct advantage which he had promptly seized. Charlie, and no doubt the chap too, had heard that the woman was a wealthy widow.

During his spell inside Charlie had endeavoured to study the French language from a book that he'd found in the prison library. But, except for a few words that he already knew anyway, picked up from hotel guests, the task had outstripped his capabilities and inclination. He found the gardening books much easier to understand and follow and much less boring. In consequence he decided that a foreign language would after all not be necessary to his plans for the future. There were plenty of English speaking widows and divorcees to be found in the right places if he should decide to pursue that course.

Then he rejected the idea altogether since he was not financially equipped to sit about in hotel foyers and lounges playing the waiting game. It all rested on luck. Could take weeks, even months. Maybe never.

He had reached the edge of the park now and sighting a bus ran to catch it as it was pulling away. The journey into town took almost an hour. He got off at the terminal and caught a local bus to Dockland.

Seven minutes later, in a hurry now, he turned the corner into the first of the maze of shabby back-streets. His first stop would be Duke Street where Lydie Collins who had been his close friend from childhood lived.

A nurse Lydie usually lived in at the nurses' quarters close to Nightingale Hospital where she worked. At present Charlie knew he would find her at home where she had been for the past two months nursing her sick mother. In her last letter to him in prison, a week ago, she had told him that the condition of her mother was deteriorating.

In Duke Street now he tapped on the door of number 10, opened it, and called as he entered — 'Hello Lydie it's me — Charlie.'

At the end of a short passageway a door opened and a pretty dark haired girl appeared. She greeted him warmly. 'Hello Charlie. It's good to see you. I'm so glad you're out of that place.'

Charlie smiled, 'Not half as glad as I am Lyd.' As he entered the tiny back room she searched his face for visible signs of his ordeal of the past six months. With relief she saw none.

'How's Mum?'

'She died two days ago.'

'I *am* sorry Lyd!'

'Do you want to see her?'

'Of course.'

Lydie led the way into the tiny front parlour, at present darkened by the lowered blind, where her mother lay in a coffin.

Charlie touched the marble-like forehead lightly with his lips. 'I'm so sorry I wasn't out in time to see her before she . . . ' His tone conveyed his genuine regret as he looked upon the waxen face. Then Lydie moved to return to the back room. Charlie followed. He flopped down onto the familiar old chintz-covered armchair beside the unlit fireplace. 'I liked your mum a lot Lyd. A proper lady she was. She was too high-class to live around here. It was a bit of a come-down for her wasn't it. Do you think she ever had any regrets?'

'No — I'm certain she did not. She and Dad were happy together. I don't believe I ever heard her laugh again after he died.' Lydie busied herself at the stove. 'I'll make us some tea.'

He watched her as she settled the kettle on the gas flames. 'You look tired Lyd. I guess you've had a few nights without sleep recently.'

'I sat up with Mum for two nights in a row. I must admit I do feel dead beat now.'

'I'll stay until after the funeral to give you a hand.'

Lydie nodded and smiled her appreciation. The kettle boiled and she made tea. 'I was about to have some soup. Would you like some?'

'You bet. I'll appreciate some decent stuff after the dishwater I've had for the past six months.'

'Have you been home yet?' Lydie ladled the soup into two willow-patterned bowls.

'Not yet. Stopped off here first to see you and collect my gear. Thanks for looking after it for me. If I'd left it round home our Ron would have been into it, and wearing my best shirts most likely.'

'Still too big for him.' Lydie eyed the broad shoulders.

'Oh he wouldn't have worried about that. My shoes would probably fit him anyway, and if they didn't he'd stuff the toes with paper.'

'He's certainly growing into a strapping lad. Soon catch you up Charlie. He's 17 next week he told me. He's excited about you coming out though. He came round to see me this morning.'

'I know. I'll have to see what I can do for him.'

They finished the soup in silence. Charlie put aside his empty bowl. 'That was good Lyd.'

'I daresay you're hungry. How would you

fancy some bacon and eggs? I've suddenly recovered my appetite. I haven't had a proper meal for days. I've lived on sandwiches.'

'Bacon and eggs sounds good to me.'

Charlie idly watched her as she worked. 'Thanks for writing to me while I was in that place Lydie. I really looked forward to those letters.'

Lydie sighed. 'I'm sorry I couldn't bring myself to visit you. I did tell you I wouldn't at the time. I was too angry at you for doing such a mad thing.'

'Mad is the right word Lyd. I wouldn't have wanted you to come to that place in any case. I told you so in my first letter; told our Ron too.'

'He used to call in to see Mum and me quite often. I believe he was lonely and needed company. Apparently he fancies living in Queensland with Fred. I think it would be a marvellous idea Charlie.'

'So do I. I always meant to pay his fare out when I have enough money to spare. He'd have a better life there. Fred is all for him going.' Charlie sniffed the air. 'Bacon smells good Lyd. Can I help?'

'You can butter the toast if you like.' Lydie put the golden crispy bread on the table in front of him as she spoke.

'Yes I'll see to it that Ron goes out there.

16

Fred's happy with the life according to his letters. I sometimes wish that I felt inclined to go myself but emigrating doesn't appeal to me.'

Lydie transferred the sizzling streaky from the pan to the plates.

'So you took time off from the hospital then? Did they give you leave or the sack?'

'Leave. I'll be glad to get back to work. I haven't been outside this door for the last two months except just to the corner shop. I telephoned the hospital this morning to let them know I'll be returning next Friday. I've written to the landlord to tell him that I'm moving out of the house.' Lydie sat down opposite Charlie. 'It really is good to have you here for the next few days until I leave. I shall need some moral support at the funeral.'

'After that you need never see this old place again.'

'It must have been hard for Mum all those years even though she never ever said anything. Do you remember when she took us to see the house where she lived as a girl?'

'Very clearly. It was the day when I secretly vowed that I'd move to a house like that. Of course looking back it would've appeared much grander to us kids than it actually was. We were comparing it to these rabbit hutches. I think your mum should have had a share of the proceeds when it was sold.'

'It wouldn't have amounted to a great deal shared out among her five brothers. Now tell me about your plans for the future Charlie. You said in your last letter that you'd made some.'

'Well, I'll be travelling up to London with you when you go. I want to find one of those high-class staff agencies. The kind that finds butlers, chauffeurs etcetera for the best houses. Only the really wealthy can afford to keep that kind of help nowadays. I'm not too concerned with how I start off. Getting established is the first step. It will have to be with the right person. I'm looking for someone oldish who hasn't got a string of descendants or relatives waiting in the wings. I shan't mind starting out as a gardener. I've learned a bit about gardening from books over the last six months. I have a driving licence — even though I haven't got a car.'

Lydie smiled and shook her head amused. How well she knew Charlie Barnes; except for what she considered was his recent mental lapse. Although she did not underestimate the potential power of his good looks and charm she knew that he was not vain for vanity's sake. He merely viewed his natural gift in the light of how it could assist him to shake off his lowly born tag. She had no doubts at all that he would achieve his goals. She had been the one who had first noticed how his handsome face attracted female attention. She had grown up with Charlie. He did not resemble either his mother, or his father who was now dead. But that was a good question — who was his real father? People had hinted that it wasn't Ted Barnes. It had been known — although not to Ted — that once, while he was away at sea, an American naval officer had stayed at the house overnight. Naval men did call in at the port and the nearest places for socialising were the corner pubs of Dockland. So the story about the naval officer was very likely true.

'Penny for them Lyd.' Charlie's voice broke into her musings.

'Oh I was just thinking about the past Charlie. What if you do find a position and discover that you don't like the people, or the person as the case may be.'

'You know me Lyd. I can handle that if it happens. I certainly won't sign any binding contracts.'

Lydie's eyes rested for a moment on his abundant brown hair in which the sun-rays always singled out gold lights, then on the distinctive arched brows above his very green eyes, and on the broad shoulders that carried his six feet of height so well. She shook her head and smiled. 'You don't look at all like a gardener or a butler Charlie. A chauffeur perhaps. Good thing you learned to drive, although you haven't had all that much experience yet.'

'Never was able to afford a car. I have driven Tyler's a few times though. Tyler's the chap who taught me.'

'Yes — I remember you mentioning Tyler. What about references Charlie? Have you considered that aspect? Suppose they find out about . . .'

'Who's to tell them?' Charlie interrupted. 'You can give me one. I can handle the rest. I shall say that I've just arrived back from Australia where I grew peaches.'

He laughed when Lydie raised her eyebrows in surprise.

'But they'll be sure to ask questions about . . .'

Again Charlie cut in. 'I've been reading all about it. I haven't completely wasted the last six months. And I do know a bit about Australia from Fred's letters.'

Charlie laid his knife and fork across his empty plate. 'Has our Ron been round here much then while I was away.'

'Quite often. He used to sit with Mum and me and talk. I was glad of his company. He's a bit of a loner. Perhaps it's just as well; liable to get in with the wrong crowd around these parts.' Lydie, now finished, started to gather up the plates.

'That was great Lyd. I'll give you a hand with the washing up before I go round home. Ron'll be waiting for me. He's not working at present.' He glanced at the mantle clock. 'I know where Ma will be until closing time. Tell you what Lyd — get Mrs Holmes next door to come in and sit for an hour or so and we'll go out and do some shopping. We'll take our Ron with us. I'll buy him a new shirt. I'll need a few things myself, and it'll do you good to get away from the house for a bit.'

Lydie took the plates from him. 'All right Charlie. But you don't have to bother with these. I've so little to do now that Mum . . . ' she glanced in the direction of the front parlour as a substitute for words.

Charlie hesitated briefly about not helping. 'Okay — if you're sure. I'll just slip upstairs and collect my things Are they still up in the back bedroom cupboard?'

In reply she nodded, then went outside to the lean-to scullery to fetch a washing up bowl.

While she waited for water to boil she went out into the yard to hang up some washing. As she did this she pondered on what Charlie had told her about his plans for the future.

She wished that he didn't have to practise deceit though — however harmless. But she hoped that he would succeed in getting what he wanted from life. Since his leaving school he had never settled long in any one place of work. Although she had thought he was quite contented in that last hotel position before the encyclopaedia-sales job. This idea of his starting out as a gardener left her doubtful. His personal appearance, although not his physique, was totally incompatible with manual labour. 'You seem to be a misfit Charlie,' she mused aloud as she pegged up the washing.

Charlie came to the back door and called, 'I'll be back in an hour Lyd.'

A moment later she heard the front door close behind him.

★ ★ ★

Lydie took one last look around the empty house. This did not take long since it consisted only of four tiny rooms and the lean-to scullery. The furniture had been disposed of, sold — practically given away, to the local second-hand dealer, apart from the few oddments to Mrs Holmes next door. Some special ornaments and good china that had been brought to the marriage by her mother she had kept and these were packed with her clothes in a suitcase. Some of the furniture had been good pieces inherited by her mother when her parental home was sold. These would be classed as antiques and sold by the dealer for a fat profit. Lydie had neither the time nor the opportunity to do this herself, and she couldn't take them with her for she had no place of her own to go to.

Tears stung her eyes as she took a last look into each empty room. Despite the humbleness, she had known happiness here with parents of the best kind. Her mother had mixed little with the neighbours in the street. Her cultured speech alone had set her apart. Charlie had liked to listen to her, and from doing so he had learned a great deal about correct English. Lydie had the same refined speech as her mother who had married a working-class man. Her only close friend had been Mrs Holmes next door, a genteel lady and a widow whose husband had become bankrupt after a failed business venture.

Lydie heard the taxi draw up outside. Brushing aside the tears she turned and closed the door for the last time on an empty silence as Charlie came to pick up her cases.

Seconds later she was beside him in the back of the car headed for the train station and London.

2

Puffing at his pipe Charlie walked briskly out of the TOFF DOMESTIC AGENCY looking distinguished in his tweeds, for which he was glad the weather had been cool enough. It had been easy and he could hardly believe his luck. A possibility first go. He put the letter of introduction into the pocket of his jacket.

'Positions for chauffeurs and butlers are becoming increasingly rare,' the woman in the agency had told him. 'But as luck would have it a lady did telephone me only this morning to say that she's in need of a gardener-chauffeur to live in as security. Apparently the man who has been in her service for the past twenty years died suddenly just over a week ago. The fact that he has stayed so long in her service does indicate that she's not a difficult person to work for. Although he did not live-in she does require his successor to do so. But . . . ' she hesitated doubtfully — 'The gardening . . . perhaps is not quite what you . . . '

'Indeed. I would be most interested,' Charlie had assured. 'It so happens that I'm extremely keen on gardening. Have been

24

since a child. Learned a great deal from my grandmother's gardener.' With secret humour Charlie had brought to mind his old grandmother, now dead, coming from the corner pub, a man's cloth cap on her head and carrying her usual jug of ale back to her tiny house with its ten feet square of backyard that hadn't a speck of soil in it.

Those gardening manuals from the prison library had been easy to follow and understand. At the time he had hoped that the hours spent memorising the plant names and their seasons might prove a good investment, if he had to start on the bottom rung as gardener. He could always refer back to books if required.

To avoid any awkward questions he had flashed the agency woman a smile showing perfect teeth, the sound condition of which owed nothing to brush and paste during childhood. He hadn't owned a toothbrush until the age of fourteen when he had bought one from his first week's wages.

The awkward questions had not come and the woman had been totally convinced by his answers to those she had asked. Then after giving him directions for finding the country house that, although a fair distance, could be reached by bus she had added, 'I'll telephone Mrs Penneston-Barkley and tell her to expect you then Mr Baines.'

Baines had been the name he'd used. He would stick to that. A genuine reference of high praise indeed from Lydie, greatly exaggerating his qualities, but true in that she had grown up with him; and the two faked ones composed and written by himself; one signed by an aristocratic sounding Major Plumworth. Charlie had given the fictitious Major's address as Moonooloo Drive — Queensland which was the home of Fred.

The other reference purported to be from a Reverend Dalton also of Queensland, 'who is in the process of moving to Western Australia and I'm awaiting his new address,' he had informed the woman at the agency. This would ensure that no check could be made. There had been a questionnaire to fill in which, he was relieved to see, bore no enquiry as to whether the applicant had a police record.

An hour and a half later, which included a change of buses and a fairly long wait between, Charlie arrived in the village of Redcliffe. The bus stopped just past the corner of Berry Lane.

At first sight he glanced about him in vague surprise, for the name had suggested a larger busier place. There were only a few shops along the main village street. In one he enquired the distance to Grandstone House in Berry Lane. 'It's a fairish way sir,' the shop owner had replied in country dialect. 'Best take a taxi unless you're fond o' walking.' Her eyes had travelled from his smoothly combed hair down to his Oxford brogues. 'It 'ud be two — mebbe three moile. Taxi just around the corner — Seven Oaks Street Ted Gilbert. Bound to be home. He's retired and it's only a side-line with him now. He'll be happy to obloige.'

Charlie thanked her and left the shop. For a few minutes he stood on the corner undecided whether or not to walk the distance to save the expense since his personal funds were rapidly diminishing. He had booked into a cheap hotel and at this stage was unsure how long his stay there would be.

The woman at the agency had informed him that the bus did not go through Berry Lane. Mrs Penneston-Barkley had advised a taxi-ride from the village, the cost of which would be her personal responsibility. She did not wish any applicant to be out of pocket. Charlie however had no intentions of allowing her to pay. Such a situation would not be compatible with the impression he wanted to project.

The sky was at present overcast and

threatening. If he took a chance and walked he would risk getting his good clothes soaked and spoiled One more calculating glance at the gathering clouds immediately overhead and he decided on the taxi.

Charlie suppressed the automatic low whistle of surprise that formed on his lips as the taxi turned the point along the fir tree lined driveway at which the house came into view. Ted Gilbert put the car brake on but left the engine running while he got out ready to open the passenger door. 'Here we are then sir.'

Charlie already out took his wallet from the breast pocket of his jacket.

Ted Gilbert looked slightly uncomfortable. 'Er — no call to pay me sir. When Mrs Penne telephoned to say she was expecting you she told me to send the account to her.'

'That won't be necessary,' Charlie insisted as he gave an enquiring look. 'How much do I — ?'

'As you wish sir.' Ted named the fare. 'Will you kindly explain to Mrs Penne then sir. I wouldn't like her to think that I hadn't taken note of her orders.'

'Will do.' Charlie knew that he wouldn't and that the man would do so himself when the time came.

As the taxi drew away Charlie walked

confidently up the steps to the impressive portico entrance and grasped the shiny brass lion-head knocker to announce his arrival.

The house surpassed anything he could have imagined or hoped for. He glanced about him and would have liked to stand back to study the sheer size of the imposing construction. He could scarcely believe his good luck in having visited that particular domestic agency and for being in the right place at the right time for once.

He knocked out his pipe against the heel of his shoe and his eyes travelled over the stretches of velvety lawns bordered by early spring flowers at each side of the house. He squared his shoulders ready to give his all to secure the position and looked forward to the challenge. With his usual self-assurance, even if so recently bruised, he convinced himself that he would be successful on account that he so desperately wanted to be. Such an opportunity as this rarely knocked twice.

He was mentally comparing the dimensions of the house with the rabbit hutches of Dockland when the door was opened by a tall middle-aged woman. He guessed she would be the housekeeper, since she looked exactly as he would have imagined the housekeeper of such a home would look. She was dressed in unrelieved black. Her iron grey hair was parted in the centre and arranged over each temple like a pair of draped curtains. Such a style would have detracted from even the most perfect features, which she certainly lacked. Her thin straight mouth created a severe expression that extended to her eyes. It was hard to imagine even the bloom of youth in its prime lending any softness to her features. Right now the only perceptible change in her expression was a slight raising of her brows on sight of him.

Charlie flashed his smile before introducing himself. 'Good morning. I'm . . . '

Before he got any further she moved back into the hall cutting short his words by saying curtly. 'Step inside.'

Charlie knew instantly that no amount of projected male charm would work on this individual; although he had sensed her surprise and knew that he was not what she had been expecting. 'This way.' She led him across the vast marble-tiled hallway to the door of the drawing room.

He shrugged off his topcoat, which he knew was the correct thing to do, and handed it to her.

With another faint raising of her brows she accepted the coat and announced him.

His shoes sank into the luxurious softness of an Aubusson carpet as he entered the room and the slight damper that the woman had cast on his spirits was instantly dispelled. For a transient moment he thought the room was deserted. Then a slight movement drew his eyes to an elderly woman on a cushioned window seat that followed the curve of the bay. He noticed a silver-handled ebony walking cane placed beside her on the seat. As she turned in his direction he saw that she wore a hearing aid. Smiling he approached her, his hand outstretched.

'Please don't get up,' he said as she grasped the walking cane and made a movement to stand. When he reached her side she extended her hand to him.

'Good afternoon Mr Baines. I'm Emily Penneston-Barkley. Briefly she turned her attention to the woman who still lingered in the doorway. 'We'll take tea now please Martha.' She returned her attention to Charlie. 'Do you prefer Indian or China Mr Baines?'

'Indian please,' he replied without hesitation in order not to show ignorance on the choice. Truth was he gave little thought to which kind of tea he drank so long as it was hot and sweet. His Ma always bought Lyons Green Label from the corner shop because she saved the stamps. But he was aware that discerning people had their preferences.

When he glanced towards the door again the woman had gone.

'Do sit down Mr Baines. There's a delightful outlook from this window.' With a sweep of her arm she indicated the garden scene and there was a brief pause while they looked out. Then with a graceful movement of her hand she patted the seat beside her and inclined her head.

'Thank you.' Charlie seated himself. His hand briefly touched the empty briarwood pipe that peeped over the top pocket of his jacket. It was one of the best available; couldn't have cheap accessories with good clothes, and he considered the pipe an important accessory. A pipe gave a chap a steady dependable air. Right now he very much wanted to project such an image. He resisted the urge to look about him but could sense the quality of his surroundings. Instead he made himself appear to be at home and unimpressed.

'My late gardener was with me for 20 years Mr Baines. He was working in the garden when he had the attack. Died on the way to the hospital I regret to say. Being married he did not live in. I own a couple of cottages in the village and he lived in one of those. After my dear husband William died I would have preferred to have a man living in for security reasons but of course I couldn't dispense with Gordon after all his years here with us.'

'I'm sure you must miss him greatly,' Charlie said for the want of some comment.

'Yes indeed — very much so.'

Charlie saw her eyes stray to the pipe and thought she was about to make some remark on it, but at that moment the woman who had shown him in entered with tea on a silver tray. She placed this on a small table close to the window seat.

'Thank you Martha.'

Even though the woman did not look his way Charlie could feel the hostility directed at him as she left the room stiffly without a word.

'Martha has been housekeeper here for 25 years. I look upon her as family really, which since the death of William consists only of myself and my young niece whom I never see because she lives in New York. Martha manages the house well with the help of a maid who comes in a couple of days a week; that's all Martha will allow. She's very possessive about her housekeeping.' She made a move to serve the tea.

Charlie instantly offered. 'Allow me.'

'Thank you Mr Baines. I'm a little clumsy at these things since my stroke.' By way of explanation she added. 'I had a slight stroke almost a year ago now. Not too incapacitating though thank heaven.'

Charlie had noticed that one side of her mouth was very slightly lopsided. 'No sugar for me thank you,' she said as Charlie proceeded to pour tea from a silver pot into rose patterned china cups. He placed one within easy reach of her hand.

'Thank you Mr Baines.'

He put two sugar lumps in his tea.

'Now about the position,' she continued, 'I trust that the agency explained the exact nature of the work. The gardening I mean . . . in addition to living in and acting occasionally as my chauffeur.'

'Yes-yes indeed. I'm very interested in gardening. I find it mind-relaxing and at the same time it fulfils a need for physical activity. I'm essentially an active person and prefer to be outdoors whenever possible. For this reason I don't care for desk work. Inactivity I find depressing.' Charlie was secretly amused. He sounded so convincing he almost believed himself.

She looked pleased and the uncertainty that her manner had suggested vanished. 'You sound so much like my dear William. He was of the same mind as you on the matter of keeping active as much as possible. I still miss him very much. A man is so much better able

34

to manage the affairs of property this size. He dealt with all the accounts and household repairs and such. The garden he particularly loved. He did some of the planting but his main interest was the greenhouses. We have twenty acres, much of which has been left in its natural wooded state. The garden part consists of a small orchard, apples, cherries, pears, and quinces. Martha makes jelly from those. Too much fruit for one household so I give a great deal of it to the hospital and the church. There's a vegetable garden, lawns, flower beds, rose gardens and the water garden — which is quite my favourite spot. As you will imagine it's all very time consuming. I can of course get extra help for the heavier digging whenever required. With regard to the chauffeuring — I go out so seldom nowadays. Just to the church in the village on Sunday for the morning service, and occasionally I dine with my friends the Wessleys who live a little further along the lane. Since William died they've been collecting me. I don't drive you see. Which is another thing I missed so much after William died. We used to go for long country drives.'

Charlie listening attentively now replaced his empty cup on the tray and leaned back against the seat. He would have felt better with his pipe in his mouth but at this point wondered if he dared. With this thought his hand strayed subconsciously to his pocket.

She noticed the movement and said, 'Please do smoke if you wish Mr Baines. I'm not one of those people who object to the smell of pipe tobacco smoke in the house. I've rather missed that. William smoked a pipe.'

'Thank you.' Charlie had noticed that her eyes had strayed a few times to the pipe bowl that rested over the top of his pocket. As he filled the pipe with tobacco from a leather pouch she continued to speak.

'I understand from the agency that you are recently returned from Australia.'

'That is correct.' Charlie proceeded to light the pipe. Meanwhile his mind was ticking over. How much information would she expect about that? He felt the steadying influence of the pipe between his teeth as he drew on it briefly before adding. 'I owned a peach orchard in South Australia for a while. Then I tried my hand at farming for a short spell. There was a prolonged drought. I lost a great deal financially. With what little money I had left I regret to say I made some very poor investments.' He paused briefly to draw again on the pipe while he searched for the right words to steer the conversation away from Australia. He liked the old girl and hated to lie to her. Besides she looked too intelligent to attempt to hoodwink too far. 'It's so good to be back in England again. I realise now that I never really could think of Australia as my home. My roots are here. Nothing quite like the English countryside or an English garden, especially the lawns. A garden is nothing without a lawn.'

'I agree. I suppose the grass must get quite parched in a hot climate.'

To his relief she did not press the subject further. She sniffed the air. 'How that reminds me of William. The first tobacco smoke in the house since he died. Now Mr Baines I should like to show you around the grounds.' With the aid of her walking cane she rose from the window seat. 'The daffodils are out at present and some bluebells in the woods.'

Charlie stood instantly to assist her by offering a supporting hand beneath her elbow.

'Thank you Mr Baines.' On the way out of the room she paused at a carved mahogany china display cabinet on which stood a silver-framed photograph of a man in hunting dress on horseback. Alongside stood a small silver bell, which she picked up and rang. The sound was musical and pleasant yet seemed as if it would echo through the quiet house.

When she replaced the bell she picked up the frame. 'This is my favourite photograph of William.' She held it out for inspection.

Charlie politely studied it for a few moments then handed it back. 'A fine-looking man. I see he has a good seat on a horse.' Although he knew nothing about four-legged transport he had heard the phrase used.

As he expected the remarks pleased her. 'Indeed Mr Baines, a very handsome man, and a very good seat. He was Master of Hounds.' She replaced the frame with care in the exact spot then moved on.

As they went out through the double oak doors into the hall Martha Oakes appeared in answer to the bell. 'We've finished now Martha thank you. I'm just going to show Mr Baines around the gardens.'

The housekeeper made no reply or comment as she passed on into the room. Again Charlie felt the hostility that emanated from the black-clad figure and sensed rather than saw a faint quizzical look in her eyes as they swept quickly over him. The thought that she might somehow know about him flashed through his mind but was dismissed instantly as too remote a possibility. According to what Mrs Penneston-Barkley had said the woman had been her housekeeper for 25 years. He doubted that she had ever strayed far from

Redcliffe during that time.

She led him to a small sewing room off the hall and through a French window that opened onto the garden. He wondered why she hadn't used the French window of the drawing room as access to the outside. As if reading his thoughts she said, 'I always come this way because it leads straight to the summer house. We can sit in there for a while until the clouds pass over. There's an excellent aspect of the gardens, especially the rose gardens, from there. I live for the garden nowadays. Very little else to fill my life.'

Once seated in the summer house she talked incessantly of the past and her late husband. To Charlie who listened politely she seemed obsessed with the past. He waited patiently for her to return to the reason for his being there. As the minutes passed his determination to secure the position increased. The idea of spending his days working in such a garden genuinely appealed to him; added to which he would live in the beautiful old house. The position was too desirable to miss out on. Besides which he really liked the old girl; nothing of a snob about her. So far she'd barely asked any questions about himself.

Eventually she rose from the white wrought-iron seat that obviously had been made specially because it followed the octagonal shape of the summer house precisely. Charlie again assisted her.

'Thank you Mr Baines. Now we'll take a walk around.' As they passed the daffodils she remarked. 'There — aren't they just gorgeous?'

'Oh to be in England . . . ' Charlie quoted. The poem was one of the few remembered from his school-days. He knew her class of society were always quoting lines of verse.

'That was one of William's favourites. He was fond of poetry.'

If I don't get this job, he thought, it won't be for the want of trying.

He offered her his arm and to his surprise she unhesitatingly accepted it with a polite response. When they had circled the rose garden and he had duly made comments on the great variety as she named each, they moved on to a sunken water-garden. For this they had to descend a few steps. 'My favourite spot Mr Baines.'

'I can see why. Such a tranquil setting. Must be especially lovely in summer.'

'It is indeed.' She indicated one of the stone seats that encircled the lily pond and fountain. 'We used to sit here — William and I. He would often read aloud to me so that we could enjoy a book or poem together.'

As Charlie assisted her up the steps she sighed for past times. From the top she paused briefly to look back. When she turned again to Charlie a gentle smile played on her lips. It was at this moment he felt confident that he had won her approval.

They continued on their tour of the garden. When they reached the garage, the door of which was closed, she made no reference to the car to Charlie's disappointment, but continued on towards the front of the house. A moment later the disappointment vanished as she asked, 'Do you hold a current driving licence Mr Baines?'

'Yes as a matter of fact I do.' His reply sounded a little too eager to his ears. Since passing his test he had kept the licence up-to-date even though he had no hopes of affording a car. 'But at present I do not have a car. Since arriving back in England I've so far had no need of one. I've been staying with a friend whose home is close to the moors. I walked a lot.'

He hoped this wouldn't pose any questions about the moors that he couldn't answer since he'd never been to any such place. On a number of occasions he had been invited by Tyler to stay at his aunt's home on the edge of the moors where he sometimes spent his summer holidays. But the opportunity had never arisen, since his summer holidays had never coincided with Tyler's.

'How very nice, at least in summer. A little draughty in winter no doubt.'

Charlie had never listened when Tyler had spoken of the moors. So in view of his limited knowledge he brought the subject easily back to cars. 'So as yet I haven't given much thought to buying a car.'

They had circled the house and returned by the sewing room entrance through which they had left. 'I shall show you over the house now Mr Baines. I'm very fond of the old place. Solid as the hills. They don't build like this nowadays.'

'I agree.' Charlie could now openly observe the interior surroundings. The furniture was a mixture of solid woods: oak, mahogany, rosewood. The floors were richly covered in Turkish and Persian rugs atop Aubusson carpets. Many large paintings hung on the walls, some old family portraits. Carved newel posts supported the turned banisters at both top and base of the wide staircase.

They made their way upstairs. Martha Oakes came from the kitchen. Unseen she stood watching them. She knew that she had seen his face before but for the life of her she couldn't for the present recall where.

Meanwhile Charlie thought that the old

lady would not be taking the trouble to lead him on a tour of the house if she hadn't already made up her mind to give him the job. The only two rooms she'd not bothered to show him were the two attic ones at the top of the house. He guessed that she didn't consider the extra climb worth the effort involved since the rooms, she informed him, were used for storage only.

They had returned downstairs. She took him into the library. With a sigh she eased herself down onto a brown embossed leather couch. 'Well Mr Baines you have now seen the house and the grounds, at least as much of the grounds as I could manage in the time. Do you still feel that you'd like to take on the responsibility for the gardens, and the weekly chauffeuring to the village church on Sunday mornings. Also take up residence here?'

He noted her expression and sensed that she was hoping he would accept the position. He also noted that she had not used either the word service, or job. It was as if she was being careful to put him on an equal level with herself, even though the employer. The interview had gone well. He could hardly even call it that since she had spoken mainly about herself and her late husband. No awkward questions had arisen that he'd not been able to handle. Even the references that he'd offered she had waved aside. He flashed her a smile and replied. 'I'd like the idea enormously.'

She looked pleased. 'I'm so glad. I shall be happy to have you live here as family just as Martha always has; although from choice she often eats in the kitchen. Meal times are lonely for me, but I can look forward to your company in the dining room now. Perhaps you can stay to dinner with us today? Or do you have to hurry back?'

'Not at all. There is no one to expect me. I'd be delighted. Thank you.'

'Excellent. Now will you just ring that little bell Mr Baines please.' She pointed to another small silver bell on the carved oak desk.

Charlie did so. Moments later like a silent genie Martha Oakes stood just inside the open doorway.

'Martha I would like you to meet Mr Baines who is going to take over the care of the gardens and also take up residence with us.'

Charlie stood up and took a few steps towards the housekeeper ready to extend a hand. 'A pleasure to meet you Miss Oakes.' And that's a bloody lie he thought as her stiff manner repelled his gesture and she ignored him completely.

'Will you arrange another setting at the dining table Martha please. Mr Baines is taking dinner with us this evening. We'll eat an hour earlier especially because he has a fairly long journey back.'

Without a word Martha Oakes turned and disappeared as silently as she had come. 'Don't be offended at Martha's off-hand manner Mr Baines. She's taciturn by nature. I'm accustomed to her ways. The only person she ever presented a different attitude to was William. I believe she was very fond of him in her own quiet way.'

'She may resent a newcomer after Gordon. Understandable of course since he was here for so long.' The incivility of the housekeeper was a novelty to Charlie. His own thought on the matter was that he'd just ignore the miserable old cat in future.

'Possibly, although she had very little to do with him. Would never even allow him to drive her to the village. On the subject of driving, the car keys are in the top drawer of that desk if you'd like to get them. It's not locked. Perhaps you'd like to drive the car back to your hotel when you leave this evening. Feel free to use it whenever you wish. It's seldom been out during the past two years since William died. Gordon drove me to the church on Sundays — that's about all. It should keep in good running order if it's used. You might even like to drive into town some evenings for a change away from the quiet here. It's only just a little over a fortnight since it was last used so it shouldn't be any trouble to start. It might be wise for you to take it for a run locally to get the feel of it before you drive back to London.'

'Thank you. I'll do that.'

'There's a local garage for petrol and they also have mechanics for repairs if the need should arise. Gordon used to prefer to fix the minor problems himself. Are you any good at that sort of thing Mr Baines?'

Charlie wondered how best to reply to this. He knew that the kind of chap he was purporting to be would proudly deny any such knowledge. Often he'd heard them; always got some mug to do the dirty work and then tell him what a clever chap he was. 'I know enough to fix minor problems. It pays to know enough in case of a breakdown on isolated roads.' This he decided was the best answer, even though in truth he knew very little, having had so little experience of cars. While he was learning to drive Tyler's car it had never given any trouble. Although Tyler had lifted the bonnet to explain a bit about the mechanical workings. 'I do think it's wise to have a little practical knowledge just in case,' he added.

'That's comforting. Although I don't anticipate any trouble. The car isn't very old and it's a reliable model. But as I don't have two sound legs nowadays I shall certainly feel easier in my mind on the journey to and from church.'

'I shall see that it's kept in good order.' Charlie's hand located the car keys as he spoke.

'Now you must feel free until dinner which will be served at six this evening specially. Wander about as you wish and choose one of the bedrooms for yourself. Oh — and remember to fill up the tank with fuel before you venture too far. I have an account with the local garage in the village. Just say Mrs Penne's account. That's the name by which I'm known. My full name is too much of a mouthful for everyday use.' She gave a light musical laugh before continuing, 'Now I must telephone the agency to thank them and ask them not to send anyone else along. See you at dinner then. Enjoy your drive.'

'Thank you.' With a smile Charlie touched his forehead in a brief semi-salute to dismiss himself, eager now to see which model of car was at his disposal. In the hall he stopped to consider the need for his topcoat which Martha Oakes had hung on the hallstand. He decided against. It wouldn't be necessary in the car. Still marvelling at his good fortune he let himself out of the house. At dinner he'd have to deliberately steer the conversation away from any mention of Australia. There was a limit to the knowledge he'd gleaned from Fred's letters, and there had been none on the subject of growing peaches; although Fred did have a couple of peach trees in his garden.

On opening the garage doors he gave a low whistle of surprise. Unobserved now he could drop his acquired image for the moment and let his natural enthusiasm show. The car was a Bentley, gleaming and obviously well cared for by the late gardener. He walked around it twice before unlocking the door on the driver's side. He ran his hands sensuously over the soft grey leather interior then read the low mileage as he seated himself behind at the wheel. For a few minutes he sat appreciating, and marvelling at his swiftly changed circumstances. His eyes travelled over the garage interior, that was large enough to house two cars, and a workbench with neatly arranged tools. Idly he wondered who had put them to use; Gordon most likely. Possibly William. A woman's old-fashioned upright bicycle rested against one wall. Must belong to the sour-faced Martha

Oakes he guessed. Mrs Penne had mentioned that the housekeeper had rejected Gordon's offers to drive her. The old bike must be her means of transport. The out-dated model seemed well suited to her image. His attention returned to the car. At the first touch of the ignition the engine purred smoothly into life. A satisfied smile settled on his lips as he backed the car out and turned it on the wide path.

Having established that the petrol tank still contained ample fuel for the present he continued along the driveway and into the lane.

Ten minutes before six o'clock which was the appointed time for dinner Charlie stood at the bay window of the bedroom that he'd chosen for himself. It overlooked the front aspect of the property and the driveway. He studied the flowers on a shallow bank that was edged by a low stone wall. Most he could recognise and name. A couple he would have to look up. No problem, there were bound to be some gardening books on those packed shelves in the library. He turned his attention back to the room that was furnished for a male guest. It contained a carved oak chest of drawers with matching tallboy, and a carved oak wardrobe, empty and waiting. The double-size bed-ends were of solid carved oak and the coverlet of jade and ivory damask. A small Persian rug was placed on the floor to one side of the bed atop a beige Aubusson carpet that reached to the bay where the polished wood floor was left uncovered. The only unmasculine item in the room was a small antique writing desk placed close to the window. A small china clock on the chest of drawers had long stopped. He set it going by his watch before wandering out into the corridor. Further along where it widened stood an enormous elaborately carved wooden storage chest that looked as if it had come from foreign parts. On this stood a small bookshelf with ebony buddha bookends holding a dozen or so books in place. He selected a volume of Burns poetry and opened the cover. On the flyleaf was a handwritten message . . . To Emily My Dearest, and there followed two lines of verse that he guessed must be from one of the poems. He replaced the book and picked out another. The Secret Garden. He flicked over the pages and saw that it was a book for children. He wondered if it was an indication that some family of Emily Penne existed somewhere. She had said that she had only a niece who lived in America. He glanced at the date of publication. No doubt the niece had visited as a child. He replaced the book and went to the head of the stairs to look over. On his return from test-driving the car he had glanced in through the open door of the drawing room. She had been dozing in a wingback armchair.

He re-lit his pipe and made his way downstairs to the dining room. Before he reached it she came into the hall. She was dressed for dinner in a lacy blouse and long black skirt 'Ah there you are Mr Baines. I trust you enjoyed your drive and that you found no problems with the car.'

'Yes I did enjoy the drive. Lovely countryside. The car is running beautifully.'

'I forgot to tell you that I usually have a pre-dinner sherry in the library each evening. A long-time habit. Dinner will be ready in ten minutes so we just have time. Perhaps you'd prefer Madeira. William always did.' In the library she indicated the bottles and glasses placed ready on a shelf. 'Will you pour please Mr Baines. I'm a little awkward since the stroke. Fortunately it affected only my left side and I'm right-handed, so it could have been worse.'

Charlie poured her a sherry, and Madeira for himself. He was not really a drinker but he knew that this was the done thing in her class of society.

'After William died I kept up the practice of

51

my pre-dinner sherry. It's so nice to have someone to join me. Martha never will.'

Martha Oakes did not sit with them for dinner even though she had been invited to.

Perhaps a bit of flattery, he thought. Compliment her on the meal? When she had left the room after serving the dinner he asked, 'Was Martha very upset over the death of Gordon?'

'If she was she didn't show it. But it's so difficult to know with Martha. One never knows what she's thinking.'

'I daresay someone new in the house may seem strange to her for a while. But she'll get used to it no doubt.'

'Faithful old retainers, especially house-keepers, often project an impression of ownership when someone new is introduced into the household. They're apt to become a little possessive of their own status. Gordon for instance behaved as though he owned the whole garden since it was mostly his own handiwork over so many years. If I'd so much as picked a flower without first consulting him I think he would have had me arrested. I once told him so.' She gave her musical laugh. 'We got on so well you see. William was the same about the greenhouse; refused to allow Gordon to have any hand in it. The three of us treated it all with good humour.'

Charlie found her an easy companion. Already he'd noted her great sense of humour. He felt pleased that they did not have the company of the sour-faced Martha Oakes at the table with them. He was determined to weave his way into the life of Grandstone House and it's owner; and no sullen-faced old cat was going to obstruct him.

Charlie placed the solid silver cutlery neatly across his empty plate, thankful that he was experienced in table etiquette; no thanks to his Ma. Lucky if you could even find a fork in the house, or even a chair not occupied with clothes or newspapers. As a child he'd sometimes sat on the paving in the backyard to eat his dinner. Back then of course he'd been quite happy with that. She never bothered about table manners and probably was not aware that any existed. To her way of thinking there were far more important considerations . . . such as enough money to supply the food in the first place, or for her glasses of stout at the corner. Occasionally, as a child, he'd been given meals at Lydie's where the table was properly set with cutlery and enough chairs to sit on. Posh he'd considered it back then.

He became aware that Mrs Penne was speaking to him.

'There have been one or two burglaries

reported in Redcliffe recently and a lawn mower stolen from someone's shed.'

'Good Lord!' There was genuine surprise in Charlie's tone as to why the devil anyone would want to nick such a cumbersome object.

'That's why I was so keen to have someone to live in as security.' She smiled. 'One gets a little nervous in one's old age.'

Martha Oakes entered to collect up the empty dishes. 'Compliments on the dinner Miss Oakes. Excellent.'

She gave no indication that she'd either heard or was interested in his opinion of her culinary skills.

Charlie considered her attitude downright churlish and he wondered that the old lady tolerated it.

When she'd left Mrs Penne reached for her walking cane that she'd hooked over the back of the dining chair beside her. Charlie rose to assist her. As they made their way across the marble floor to the drawing room she sniffed the air ecstatically. 'Ah! The smell of pipe smoke puts the clock back for me. How well I recall that it always seemed to linger in the hall.'

Silently he thanked providence that her much missed William had been a pipe smoker. From this element of the past she attempted to resurrect his presence.

In the drawing room he saw her seated before taking the gentleman's wingback opposite her. She talked a great deal. Perhaps the release of so much stored unspoken thought with no ears to listen since William's death, for the uncommunicative housekeeper appeared to live in a detached morose world of her own.

During the next hour very little reference to his own life was made and no questions asked that he could not readily answer. It appeared that she was more than satisfied to take him at his face value. He found her surprisingly youthful minded, and with her ever-present sense of humour a pleasant companion despite her age.

'William and I used to give a great many dinner parties when we were younger. I must arrange one soon so that I can introduce you. My very close friends and neighbours the Wessleys come to dine occasionally. Alice — Mrs Wessley — sometimes calls in of an afternoon for a chat. But as a rule she's kept busy with her charity work. They have a son Clive. He's a Scotland Yard detective. Such a nice boy; I still think of him as that although he must be thirty now. I've known him since he was a small boy.'

A detective! Charlie felt a pang of unease.

As a very close friend Clive Wessley would have her interests in mind and naturally be inquisitive and suspicious. He might not swallow the story about Australia and could possibly decide to make a few enquiries to satisfy curiosity. Detectives were never off duty. 'Scotland Yard you say? I dare say that he's kept pretty busy and away from home a great deal?'

'Afraid so. Now and again he manages a nice quiet weekend at home. He always calls in to see me. He was here for Gordon's funeral.'

'Have you any relatives living close?' He wanted to recap on what she'd said earlier about having only a niece in America. Also he was unsure of how to address her. As she had already remarked her name was a bit of a mouthful. He puffed on his pipe calmly to give the impression of being relaxed and attentive, giving no indication of the close attention with which he awaited her replies.

'To my regret William and I were not blessed with children. My only living relative now is my niece whom I spoke of earlier. She lives in New York. I've not seen her since she and her mother came on a visit eleven years ago. She's the daughter of my late sister Eileen who died only six months ago. There was a twenty-year age gap between us. She

56

married an American and went to live in New York twenty-four years ago after a whirlwind courtship. During that time Eileen visited us three times and on each occasion brought Paula with her. The first time was when she was a baby about eleven months old. Again at the age of seven and the last visit when she was about twelve years old. I believe the marriage was not a happy one. I think Paula has no relatives there from her father's side. At least none that she's ever seen or been in contact with. I know my sister always hankered to return to England. Even after so long she always referred to England as home in her letters to me. But Paula never wanted to come here to settle and of course that prevented Eileen from doing so. She died of a terminal illness. Paula's father is also dead now. A road fatality — before the death of Eileen. Apparently there was a woman in the car with him at the time of the crash and she died also. After their deaths Eileen discovered that the woman had a daughter by him, a couple of years older than Paula. So they must have known each other before he met my sister in England. I don't know the full story of the association. Anyway Eileen never did manage another visit to England before she died.'

'Is your niece planning to visit you?'

57

'I wish I really knew. She has written a few times since the death of her mother, always with promises to come when she can get away. She seems terribly involved with her work. She knows about my stroke. We still exchange letters. Fortunately I can still write despite the stroke. I always live in hope that she'll consider making her permanent home here at Grandstone House. It will be hers someday. I'd like to think it will stay in family hands. My dearest wish is that she will come to visit and decide that she loves the old place as much as I. Yet too much to hope for I expect. She most likely would find it too quiet for her after life in New York. Also it would mean having to give up her work — whatever it is. I have of course reminded her in my letters that London is not really so very far away. But it's probably all wishful thinking on my part. I have a feeling that she never will come to live permanently. To think that Grandstone House will be sold after I'm gone makes me sad.'

'I'm surprised she doesn't visit. One would think she'd be keen to get away from the noise and pollution of New York and spend some time in the English countryside. Especially here on this lovely estate. I prefer the quietude. I certainly wouldn't dream of ever parting with such a wonderful old house if I were in her place. Perhaps she may feel that way about it eventually. Plenty of time yet.' Charlie puffed at his pipe. She watched him, a smile of satisfaction on her lips. When she had contacted the agency she hadn't expected someone quite like him. Sincere, dependable looking, distinguished, and astonishingly handsome.

3

In his cheap hotel Charlie was up early. As he made a list of things that he would need for Grandstone House he whistled softly, well satisfied with providence for having directed his feet to THE TOFF DOMESTIC AGENCY at the opportune time.

Would he be expected to supply his own bathroom linen? He wondered about laundry arrangements too. He couldn't imagine anything so mundane as washday taking place there. He supposed sour-faced Martha did it. Or perhaps they employed a laundry-maid. He folded the shirts counting them once again. He considered whether perhaps he should buy just one more. These had been bought on the day of his release when he, Lydie and Ron had gone shopping. He stopped whistling briefly and frowned in concentration. Yes, he would buy just one more shirt. He ticked off several items on the list. A new suitcase; he couldn't arrive with his old battered second-hand one. He would need one before he could pack. The shops were only five minutes walk away.

On the journey back to Grandstone House

in the Bentley next morning Charlie sang softly to himself. He had telephoned Lydie to tell her of his good fortune. He would write to his Ma and Ron later.

More than content with his new lot he put the car away in the garage and took his packed suitcase from the boot. He could still smell the leather interior of the car clinging to his clothes. He entered the house by a side door with a key selected from the bunch provided by Emily Penne for his own personal use. After hanging his topcoat on the hall-stand he glanced in the drawing room intending to announce his return. She was not there.

He carried his case upstairs to his bedroom and unpacked his belongings. When he came from the room to go downstairs he saw Martha Oakes just ahead on the landing dressed in her black old-fashioned outdoor clothes.

'Good morning Miss Oakes. The weather looks promising today.'

She did not react to his greeting and completely ignored his weather report. Without so much as a backward glance in his direction she continued on her way with a begrudged, 'Good morning' and did not acknowledge him by name.

Although only very brief, her presence cast

a distinct gloom on him. He shrugged this off and went downstairs in search of Mrs Penne before making his preliminary inspection of the garden and grounds prior to starting work. He met her in the hall as she came from the sewing room. 'Good morning.'

On seeing him she smiled with pleasure. 'Good morning Mr Baines. What lovely weather. I've just been for a short turn around the garden. I expect you've just passed Martha. It's her day off. I say day because it's supposed to be but she never stays away from the house for very long. She'll be back again just after lunch as usual I expect and will have left something cold for our midday meal.'

'Should I have offered to drive her?'

'Oh no. She prefers to ride her old bicycle. Only goes as far as her sister's cottage in the village. I'm so pleased that you could make a start immediately and do so hope that the garden hasn't suffered too much during the past two weeks of neglect. I'll take a walk around with you so that we can decide what needs attention first. A few weeds have sprung up among the roses.'

So began the new life that Charlie had mapped out for himself.

A monthly salary had been agreed upon which Mrs Penne had insisted on paying in advance. The sum was equivalent to that which she had paid his predecessor and he would be living as family at no financial cost to himself. His weekends were free except that he would be required to drive her to church and back on Sunday mornings. The car he could make use of as he wished.

The garden presented no problems. The knowledge that he'd gained from studying the books on garden maintenance paid off. Any uncertainties about particular plants or procedures he covered by asking for specific instructions regarding the methods that had been used by her late gardener. 'I want to continue to maintain everything in exactly the same way so that nothing changes. Long experience made him an expert. He probably knew every worm in the soil personally.'

She had given her light musical laugh at that and given him the information he required. In establishing an invisible contact between himself, her late gardener and her dead husband by referring to them by name during their conversations, he felt confident that she would readily accept and involve him as an essential part of life at Grandstone House.

Charlie was not an expert gardener — but he was certainly an expert charmer.

On Saturday afternoon Charlie took the car into town to collect Lydie and take her to a theatre for a matinee performance of The Mouse Trap. He had telephoned her from the house during the week to arrange this. She was on night duty at the hospital this week and was free during the day.

'Charlie!' She showed her surprise on seeing the Bentley when he collected her from the nurses' quarters. She settled herself in the front passenger seat. 'It's beautiful! I'm surprised that you're allowed to have personal use of it.'

'Well the old lady practically insisted that I should take it and go to see a show in town. She's afraid I might get bored with the quiet and no young company. I've really landed on my feet Lyd.'

'I'm pleased for you Charlie. I hope you're managing with the gardening. It seems strange you doing work like that.'

'I'm enjoying it. I feel really free when I'm digging and planting, and mowing the lawns. Mrs Penne's a nice old girl.'

'Mrs Penne? I thought you said she had a double barrelled name.'

'I did. But apparently she's known as Mrs Penne for convenience. You must come to the house and meet her some time Lyd. I know you'd like her.'

'I'm certain of it. Didn't she question the references at all? Or the other things you told her — about living in Australia?'

'No. She talks mainly about her own life, especially the time before her husband died. She was very fond of him it seems.'

'I do like the sound of her Charlie and I'd like to see the house one of these days. From what you've told me it's the kind of place you've always wished you owned yourself.'

'It is. Let's face it Lyd this is the only way I'm ever likely to.'

'Has she no relatives then?'

'Apparently a niece in America who evidently couldn't care less about the place — or about her. At least she never comes to visit.'

'Well let's hope she stays away. I hope you find what you want from life there Charlie. For now we'll just enjoy the afternoon. I'm quite looking forward to the play and a few hours away from the hospital.'

4

'I think it must be almost time for lunch Charles.'

In the garden warmed by May sunshine the old lady sat on a bench watching Charlie at work. This had been his own suggestion. 'Better than sitting all by yourself at the window,' he'd told her when he saw what a lonely existence life was for her. He didn't wonder at her need to cling to the past since her William had died. He began to understand why she spoke so incessantly of her life with him, also the extent to which she missed him.

He glanced at his watch and straightened up. 'So it is.' He rested the secateurs on a pile of clippings in the barrow and knocked out his pipe and placed it in the top pocket of his shirt. He crossed the grass to where she was seated. 'Ready then?' He offered his arm and she stood up with the aid of her walking cane. They walked together across the freshly cut lawn to the French door of the sewing room, which was their usual access to the garden. She sniffed the air. 'It would be difficult for me to decide which I like most — the scent of newly cut grass or the scent of the roses.'

'Me too,' he agreed.

She had quite naturally during that first week slipped into the habit of calling him by his Christian name. One evening at the dining table she'd said, 'Please call me Emily. Gordon always did.'

'I notice that Martha never does,' he'd remarked.

Emily Penne had given her usual laugh, 'No. That's true. She's always insisted on calling me Mrs Penne. Out of sheer cussedness I suspect. Yet strangely she always called William by his Christian name. Gordon always used to call him Will. Formality seems quite out of place when one knows a person so well. William disliked formality. He was very easy going.'

Charlie had been pleased with the early headway to familiarity that came naturally due to her warm and friendly manner, with no contrivance from himself.

When they reached the French door he handed her up the step before bending to remove his gardening shoes to change into those placed ready just inside the room.

He went to the cloakroom to first wash his hands, then upstairs to his bathroom. This had been allocated for his sole use and was situated close to his bedroom. As he tidied himself up he was whistling softly. Never in his life before had he felt so contented and happy. He was enjoying the work. It wasn't even hard. All the hard work had been done years ago. Only constant attention was necessary now to maintain the perfect order of the garden and estate.

Smiling at life, which was being more than kind to him he flicked a comb through his thick hair. Surely nothing could go wrong now to spoil things. Still whistling he went downstairs to join Emily Penne for lunch in the breakfast room.

★　★　★

On Saturday morning during breakfast Emily Penne asked, 'Will you be going into the city today Charles?'

'Yes. Thought I'd take a trip in this afternoon and later have dinner with an old friend. But how would you like to go for a drive this morning?'

'That's very thoughtful of you. I'd love to if you're sure it wouldn't be imposing on your time. After all Saturday is supposed to be your day off.'

'It'll be a pleasure. We'll go as soon as you like.' He hadn't planned to start out on his own pursuits until after lunch. He had arranged to meet Lydie and take her to a show and a meal somewhere; she was on early shift and not off duty until afternoon.

'I can be ready in fifteen minutes then.' Emily Penne sounded eager at the idea of a drive. 'I'd better let Martha know I'm going out.' As she spoke Martha Oakes entered the room to collect up the breakfast dishes.

'I'm going out for a drive Martha. So take a key with you in case I'm still out when you get back from the village.'

Charlie threw a quick glance at the face of the housekeeper and noted that faint raising of her eyebrows in silent response.

Twenty minutes later he handed the old lady into the front passenger seat.

As he seated himself behind the wheel she smiled with pleasure. 'Seems quite like old times when William and I used to go on country drives.'

When they drove through the gate she continued, 'Martha likes to take her time when she goes into the village on Saturday mornings. She calls in to see her sister.'

'Well I hope she's more talkative to her sister than she is to us.'

Emily Penne chuckled, 'Yes I hope so too.' On the old-fashioned upright Martha Oakes pedalled at her usual steady rate along the lane. Her malevolent thoughts were at present on Charlie. Something not quite right about him. He was not the usual kind who took on such work. The old fool should know that. Why had he applied for the position? Something not quite above-board about it. On top of which his face was familiar. Ever since his arrival memory had nagged persistently. Certainly a face that one would remember. Yet she never went any further than the village and to the cinema in the town on Friday evenings. Perhaps that was it, the cinema, some actor whom he resembled. But who? She couldn't bring anyone to mind. It was glaringly obvious that he was trying to insinuate himself into the household and sucking up to the silly old fool. As if she hadn't always had too much attention. Spoiled all her life until William died. Gordon hadn't lived-in. Why this one? Security indeed! And look at the way he dressed; expensive tweeds. Just like William used to wear. He'd looked good in them too. Her thoughts lingered on the memory of William Penniston-Barkley. Her mind recalled the time when she had first come to work at Grandstone House as a live-in housemaid at the age of 35. He had been 46 then. He'd been the only man whom she had ever fallen in love with. In all those years neither he nor his wife suspected. It had been a one-sided secret.

When she reached the end of the lane she crossed over the main street of the village and turned down a side lane. She parked the old upright outside the small terrace cottage where her sister lived. Her dark musings had returned to Charlie as she knocked on the door and let herself in.

★　★　★

On Sunday morning as Charlie was preparing to drive Emily Penne to the church he wondered whether she would expect him to attend the service too. No mention had so far been made as to whether Gordon had been in the habit of doing so, or if he had dropped her off and returned to collect her when the service was over. 'It'll please her if I do attend,' he told his reflection in the bathroom mirror as he checked his fine moustache that he'd just trimmed. With this decision he went to his bedroom to dress for church.

As they took their places in the front pew all eyes focussed on them, or at least on Charlie, who noted that Emily Penne looked amused and pleased.

'I shall have a few questions to answer after the service,' she whispered. 'But I shan't embarrass you. I shall merely introduce you as my guest. Eventually you'll be known as the guest who stayed on. At least I hope so,' she chuckled.

Charlie smiled back at her. Her sense of humour was always in evidence. He knew that she had been delighted at his decision to accompany her for the service.

During the sermon his mind wandered back to the last time he'd attended a church service. A long way back . . . when he was 12 years old, with Lydie. On several occasions before that she had coaxed him into attending a service with her and he'd done so only to please her. But on that last particular day he had refused on account that the seat was out of his only pair of pants. However hard he'd tried to take care of his clothes they got shabby and worn-out fast. He now knew that the reason had been their cheapness. His Ma had little money to spend on his clothes, although she always managed to find enough for her glass of stout at the corner. It had been the prospect of seeing the choirmaster, who according to Lydie had pink eyes and could not see well by day, that had outweighed his concern about the missing rear portion of navy blue flannel.

At the vivid recollection a smile played on his lips. Lydie it seemed could tell bigger ones than he if it suited her purpose. Or had she really believed that story about the white haired choirmaster? Only now on reflection, so many years later, did he realize that the chap was probably an Albino. What had happened next had obliterated all desire to see the pink-eyed man from his mind.

During the service Charlie had experienced shame and humiliation. Two boys of his own age in the pew behind whispered together before calling across in voices that he feared would be heard above the volume of 70 singers, plus the organ . . . 'Hey nipper — your arse is showing.'

Beside him Lydie had turned round angrily on the boys. 'What's the matter haven't you seen an arse before! You've got one haven't you. Or has your mother cut if off like she's always saying she will!' This unlikely threat from some demented parent was often heard in the vicinity of Dockland, although never in the house of young Lydie. Anger had been responsible for her lapse. Then reaction at her own uncharacteristic outburst sent her into a fit of giggling. This triggered off the same response in the boys and threatened to spread amongst the younger members of the congregation. This went on amidst withering looks from their elders. Lydie had stuffed her handkerchief into her mouth in an attempt to stifle her laughter. Charlie had remained straight faced and tight to his seat throughout the rest of the service, ever-ready with the excuse that he had cramp in his legs if the vicar should notice, and lacking the courage to steal out of the church when all eyes were closed. During the last prayer, driven by desperation, he had made a speedy exit along the aisle with one hand clamped over the offending gap that to Charlie, in his present state of mind, was at least ten times larger than in reality.

Now as he reflected on that humiliating day in another church he glanced down at his immaculate pants. Perhaps his burning ambition for only the best had begun then and been fostered throughout the following years when he'd been in need, at times of only a needle and thread.

'We will all kneel,' commanded the sonorous voice from the pulpit. Once again Charlie would rather have kept to his seat; this time merely in order not to spoil the creases down the length of his pants and cause them to sag at the knees. Couldn't see much sense in compulsory kneeling, could pray just as well standing. Carefully he sank to his knees onto the hassock. His bent head screened the faint smile that played at the corners of his mouth. He was recalling that ten-year-old Lydie had supplied the required needle and thread that same day. From a pair of her father's old trousers destined for the ragbag she had cut a patch which did not quite match his torn ones but at least was navy blue. Then under the guiding instructions of her mother she had bridged the offending gap.

While she had carried out the patchwork Charlie, dressed in the much over-sized pants temporarily reprieved from the ragbag, had cavorted about like a clown to amuse them.

Later when his Ma had eventually noticed the patch she had bawled at him, 'You bloody monkey getting other people to mend y' clothes! What'll they think! I'll do the mendin' when it's needed!'

Charlie had wanted to answer back, 'Why don't you then?' But had known this would only bring about a clip round the ear and no purpose served.

The deep musical voice from the pulpit again broke into his thoughts. 'We will all rise.' With great relief Charlie promptly complied.

One afternoon about two weeks later Charlie carried a rattan armchair from the sewing room into the sunlit garden for Emily Penne to sit more comfortably while she watched him at work.

'Softer than the bench Charles,' she said as

she sank back onto the cushions. 'You're so thoughtful.'

An hour later he saw that she had dozed off to sleep.

Martha Oakes had gone into the village and would no doubt be calling on her sister. She would be gone at least an hour. For such an opportunity he had been waiting. He put aside the hoe and went into the house. If Emily Penne awoke during his short absence she would assume that he'd gone to the bathroom. He ran upstairs two at a time and went into her bedroom. In a small antique bureau there was a key in the lock. He turned this and opened the flap. The contents were stored neatly and he instantly saw a bundle of letters with red and blue striped borders. He picked up the bundle and briefly studied the American postmarks. From beneath the pale blue tape that secured them he slipped out the top letter and crossed the room to stand at the window from which point he could see Emily Penne still napping. He opened the letter and read . . .

Dear Aunt Emily

Prepare yourself I have very sad news. Mother died yesterday in hospital where she has been for the past two weeks. I'm so sorry that she never did make it to England to visit you. *She had been hoping to spend Christmas with you — it was where her heart always was you know, even after all these years. She often spoke of Redcliffe and Grandstone House. So now I am alone. I have no relatives here that I know of. I believe there may have been an uncle of sorts living in Arizona but I don't have an address and have never seen him. Father once made some reference to a cousin but never kept in touch with him. So apart from yourself there is no one to notify. I am kept extremely busy with my work so don't have time to dwell on my grief. I shall sell mother's house. As you know I have been renting an apartment closer to my work for some while now. I did however take time off and move back home with Mother when she was first taken ill. I shall be returning to my apartment after the funeral. I can't at present see my way free enough to come on a visit but I shall as soon as I'm able ...*

Charlie read no further and moved on to the next bundle.

Dear Aunt Emily
    Mother was taken ill yesterday and is in hospital. She asked me to be sure and let

you know. I've been at home looking after her for three weeks now. Her condition got suddenly worse. The doctor says that she's been neglecting herself by not consulting him sooner. I shall write to you again in a few days with — I hope — better news. Your loving niece Paula.

Charlie replaced the letter and extracted another at random. His eyes scanned the pages reading only snatches for signs that might indicate just how likely a visit from the writer might be.

. . . James . . . my boss . . . married to an awful woman . . . alcoholic . . .

Charlie smiled in amusement having deduced that the niece was probably having an affair with the chap and his wife wouldn't agree to a divorce. Sounds promising, he thought as he replaced the letter. With a love attachment to keep her in New York there was less chance of her visiting. He took a letter from the bottom of the batch since the letters were in order of date written. As he unfolded the pages a small snapshot fell out and landed face downwards on the floor. When he picked it up and turned it over he saw that it was a full-length picture of a girl who looked about 13 to 14 years of age. After a cursory glance he put it aside and began to read the letter.

Dear Aunt Emily

It's as well that I'm left-handed or I shouldn't be able to write this letter to you today. I sprained my right wrist yesterday. Just my luck! I was supposed to be playing in the tennis tournament today at school so I'm feeling awful mad at myself.

Charlie replaced it in its envelope with the snapshot. Little point in reading anything so far back in time. As he restored the bundle to its place he caught sight of another beneath an accounts book. A hasty look at the opening words and the signature on the last page revealed that this pile was from Emily Penne's sister. Again — no point in reading these, for the writer was dead. He re-locked the bureau and returned to the garden. As he took up the hoe Emily Penne awoke and continued speaking as if unaware of her recent catnap.

Gradually they fell into the practice of taking a walk around the garden after dinner, weather permitting, to look at the results of Charlie's efforts. The rest of the evenings they spent in the drawing room either playing chess or listening to music. At times Charlie would read aloud to her. There was little else outside the home to occupy a quiet country evening other than a long drive to the city.

This evening as they left the dining room after dinner Emily Penne remarked. 'I have the tiresome task of attending to the household accounts Charles. I have to admit that I'm not very efficient or business-like in these matters. William always attended to that sort of thing. I paid the rates twice by mistake last year and wasn't aware of it until the cheque sent in error was returned to me.'

'If I can assist in any way you have only to ask,' Charlie offered readily.

'Yes of course I do know that but I feel that I already impose on your free time, evenings and Saturday morning drives, and church on Sundays. You're young and should be out mixing with people of your own age not squandering your time on an old woman.'

'Actually I really do enjoy the evenings spent at home.' This was quite true. It was the life of which he had always dreamed. He already felt as if he was the master of the big old house and surrounding estate. And she certainly always treated him as if he were. As for the daytime work he was more than happy with that, he had never felt so fit. The sunshine had given him a healthy looking skin and erased any taint left by half a year in captivity. Living as a privileged class now he had put the ugly past behind him as if it had never been. He looked forward to the promising future.

They had reached the French door of the drawing room and as he opened it he saw that a fine misty rain had started.

'Oh well — no walk this evening Charles.' They turned back into the room. When she was seated Charlie lit his pipe and gave three draws on it before reiterating . . . 'Yes I enjoy the evenings at home.'

'I'm so glad. But I want you to promise me that if you're short of money and need something you'll let me know. I'm not saying this lightly Charles. Please remember that.'

He smiled as if indulging her. 'I will. Now about these household accounts. Lead me to them and they're as good as done.'

'Are you certain Charles. I'd be so very grateful. Actually most are still unopened on the hall table.' She chuckled. 'I rather suspect there'll be a few final notices among them. I'm afraid I do tend to put off the job. The chequebook is in the bottom drawer left of the desk in the library. Thank you so much. Meanwhile I can spend the evening writing to my niece. It's about time I sent another letter. I haven't told her about you yet. And you might just be the bait to bring her over on a visit.'

Charlie smiled politely in response although he didn't feel happy at the idea. She could be right. Curiosity might bring about a visit. He would rather that any competition for the old lady's affection and interest was a few thousand miles away in America. 'I'll bring in the cheques for you to sign.' At the door he paused to look back and add, 'From now on consider the accounts to be my job.' Puffing contentedly on his pipe he gathered up the unopened mail from the mahogany table in the hall and went off towards the library.

When he next received his monthly pay-cheque he saw with surprise and delight that she had doubled his salary. The cheque was always left in a sealed envelope for him on the desktop in the library.

Martha Oakes continued her distant manner towards him. The glances of suspicion and disapproval had long since ceased to bother him. By now he had concluded that she had no power to influence Emily Penne with her opinions. After the first two weeks at Grandstone House he had stopped trying to win her over; she was impervious to any friendly approaches.

'Why don't you invite Lydia over to dinner with us one evening Charles? I can invite the Wessleys. They're back from holiday now. Alice phoned earlier to let me know they've returned and that Clive will be home for the weekend. Be nice to make up a small dinner party.'

Emily Penne watched his strong muscular body as he dug over the earth with a gardening fork. He stopped digging and straightened up to look across to where she sat in the wicker chair. 'I'm sure she'd be delighted. What about Saturday — she's not on duty.' With the back of his hand he pushed back a lock of hair that clung to his damp forehead. At the mention of Clive Wessley, whom he had as yet not met, his old doubts surfaced. Sooner or later he would have to meet the chap and perhaps this might be easier with Lydie there to absorb some of the attention. She was damn good-looking and well able to mix easily with the upper class society; thanks to her mother who had taught her to speak decent English from the beginning. Through them both he had discovered the distinction himself.

Emily Penne looked pleased. 'Saturday will be perfect. Will you telephone her later and arrange to collect her?'

'Will do.' Charlie stepped from the vegetable bed that he was preparing for planting. 'I think I should go and fetch the garden umbrella for you. It's a bit hot today in the full sun.'

'Thank you Charles. It is rather.' She

watched him cross the lawn to the garden shed. He had told her about Lydie Collins and their long close friendship. 'Are you planning to marry her?' she had asked him and with amusement been assured, 'Good heavens no! Our friendship is purely platonic. We grew up together. Lydie lived in the next street from me. We're like brother and sister.'

'How nice,' she had replied, pleased that she was not to lose him so soon to a wife. 'Friendships like that are rare indeed.'

★ ★ ★

During dinner on Saturday evening, to Charlie's relief, no awkward questions arose. The conversation touched only on the subjects of the garden, the hospital work of Lydie and Clive Wessley's plans during his well earned weekend break. Home to relax from the pressures of his work Clive resisted voicing the curiosity which came as second nature to him; although it had been invoked at the sight of Charlie. He had been told in advance of Emily Penne's recently employed live-in gardener.

She had offered no information on the matter except to say that Charlie was Gordon's successor and was resident in the house for reasons of convenience and security.

The Wessleys had known in advance of her intentions to engage someone to take over after the death of Gordon. 'You're keen on gardening then Charlie?' Clive Wessley asked.

'Yes indeed. I prefer an active life. I'd get much too restless with desk work I'm afraid.'

'I can appreciate that. I'm just the same. Fortunately I don't have to spend all my time at headquarters. I'm out and about a fair bit.'

Charlie had noticed that Clive Wessley's eyes lingered on Lydie frequently during the evening. He saw too that she was well aware of this. With secret amusement he had noted also that the detective had managed in an indirect way to discover what the exact relationship was between Lydie and himself.

When Emily Penne had been told that Lydie was off duty for the whole of Saturday and Sunday she had invited her to stay over for the weekend. Lydie had been delighted to accept.

Towards the end of the evening when they were all assembled in the drawing room Clive Wessley asked, 'Do either of you ride at all? I have a couple of decent horses and wondered whether you both might perhaps join me for an hour or so after breakfast tomorrow morning?'

Politely Charlie declined the invitation. He knew in any case that it was Lydie's company that Clive desired and his own wouldn't be pressed for. 'You go Lydie.' He could see that she was quite taken with the chap. Might turn out to be her big chance.

'I'd love to but I'm afraid that I've never ridden a horse before.'

'Then now is the time to start,' Clive Wessley persisted. 'I'll give you your first riding lesson.' He threw a look of enquiry to Emily Penne. 'If you won't mind?'

'Of course Lydie should go. You're not home often enough and must make the most of the opportunity.'

While Lydie considered this her eyes rested on Clive. There was a calm air of strength and dependability about him, quite apart from his tall muscular build, and she felt sure she would have no last minute qualms about the horses. 'Thank you. I'd like to.'

★   ★   ★

Lydie now spent all her free weekends at Grandstone House. On most of these Clive Wessley also managed to be off duty nowadays. It had by now become the practice for them to go riding for an hour or so when the weather was fine. Often he stayed to dinner. He also took her to his home Tanglewood, a few miles further on along the lane, to meet his parents Alice and John Wessley.

'I haven't seen so much of Clive for years,' Emily Penne laughed. 'He obviously has no problems arranging time off when Lydie is here. I'm so glad. It's wonderful having young people in the house. You all brighten up my life so much. It all seems too good to last.'

'No reason why it shouldn't.' Lydie kissed her on the cheek. 'I love being here.'

5

Even though the September morning was warm and sunny Emily Penne had not come out into the garden as she usually did. From where he was dead-heading the roses Charlie kept glancing across to the French door of the sewing room through which she always made her appearance. It was almost time for morning tea now and still she hadn't shown.

Puzzled he put down the secateurs and made his way towards the sewing room. At the French door he changed into his leather indoor moccasins and went through into the hall. With surprise he watched the doctor coming down the stairs.

'Ah there you are Charlie,' the doctor greeted him. 'Emily asked me to come and find you. She wants you to go up to her room.'

'Is she ill then doctor? I had no idea!'

'Seems she's caught a chill. Best that she stays in bed for a day or so. I've left a prescription. Perhaps you'll collect it from the chemist. I'll look in again on Friday. Meanwhile if you're at all anxious about her condition don't hesitate to call me.'

'Of course Doctor.' Charlie started up the stairs. Martha appeared and he heard the doctor say, 'Now Martha I shall need to give you some instructions regarding Emily's diet for the present.'

The door to Emily Penne's room stood wide open and she was watching for his arrival. As he raised his hand to knock she called, 'Come in Charles.' On seeing him she brightened. 'Sit down.'

He crossed the room and seated himself on a chair beside the bed. 'Martha never told me you were ill! I've just passed the doctor. I was on my way in to see why you hadn't come out.'

She adjusted her hearing aid. 'Can you spare an hour away from the garden? The weather looks so nice. I shall miss coming out.'

'Yes of course I can. I wish Martha had told me. I did wonder why you didn't come down to breakfast.'

'Actually I did ask her to let you know that I wasn't feeling too bright. I suppose she must have forgotten. Well never mind. Now what I want to ask you is whether you'd mind writing a letter for me to my niece after you've had your morning tea? I had planned to write today and want to get a letter off without delay but don't feel up to it. I can dictate it to you. Will you mind Charles?'

'Not at all. Just tell me where I can find the notepaper and I'll do it right away. Morning tea can wait.' Actually he already knew where the special notepaper was that she always used for her letters to America. He had noticed it in the bureau the day he'd glanced through the letters from her niece.

'In the bureau,' she pointed. 'It's not locked.'

'Right. I'll just slip along and wash my hands. I came straight up from the garden.'

She nodded then said, 'But I insist that you have your morning tea before writing the letter.'

At the door he turned and smiled, 'Right. Back in fifteen minutes then.'

★   ★   ★

Charlie sealed down the envelope. 'If I leave now I'll be in time to catch the post.' He picked up the prescription slip from the bedside table. 'I'll collect this at the same time.' He was not too chuffed with the contents of the letter that she had dictated to him. It would almost certainly bring her niece Paula running to her side. He had toyed with the idea of wording it in less urgent terms but decided against this in case she asked him to

90

read it back to her when finished. It had occurred to him that he could rewrite it before mailing but only one sheet of paper remained on the pad. There was he noticed an unopened box of the notepaper in the bureau but access was not possible without her notice. There was no alternative but to post the letter in its present form and hope that Miss Paula Carpenter was still unable or unwilling to make the visit to her aunt.

Charlie didn't want his own position in the old lady's life usurped. He knew that she'd grown fond of him already, in a maternal way. The niece would of course inherit Grandstone House. He hated the thought that in consequence it would be sold when that time came.

6

NEW YORK

Paula Carpenter frowned as she studied the strange handwriting on the familiar pale grey envelope bearing an English postmark before tearing it open.

Alarm sent her mind racing ahead on possibilities why a stranger should be writing from Grandstone House. She knew the writing was not that of Martha Oakes.

At the time of Emily Penne's stroke Martha had written the letter giving the news. Small handwriting — not this large bold style. She relaxed as she read the opening words.

Paula Dear

Charles is writing this letter for me. I'm sure you won't mind my dear, since I have mentioned him in my recent letters he will not seem a stranger to you . . .

The frown still remained when she came to the end of the letter and glanced at her aunt's signature.

'Anything wrong honey?' James Maddison noted her expression as he went to pour some drinks from a decanter on the cocktail cabinet. They had just arrived at Paula's apartment having finished work at the offices of Maddison's Enterprises for the day.

'Afraid so. It seems that my aunt was too ill to write this herself so got her Mr Baines — her Charlie — to do it.' She handed him the pages as he placed two glasses of wine on a coffee table.

'You don't say! That guy who works for her?'

She nodded as he took the letter and read it through before making any comment. 'Well he's sure gotten himself well in her favour. She says she's confined to bed. So he must have written it in her room. Can't get much more familiar than that!' He too was frowning now.

'I guess you're right. Why didn't she get Martha Oakes to write it? I don't like the implications. Haven't since she first wrote to say he was living in the house for security reasons.'

'Well I guess that was around six months ago. Surely your aunt would have discovered by now if he couldn't be trusted.'

'I don't mean that exactly James. I haven't mentioned this before but I have wondered whether he has some ulterior motive for being there. From my aunt's description he doesn't strike me as the sort who normally takes on that kind of employment. Gardening I mean. And it isn't only that — he appears to have taken over her personal responsibilities. She mentioned in her last letter that he'd assumed the task of dealing with the household accounts for her. I really don't like the sound of it at all.'

'Now honey you can't think he's after marriage! Your aunt's old enough to be his grandmother! Didn't you tell me he was a young guy? Surely she'd be well past such ideas herself by now. Maybe he just has a penchant for gardening —'

'No,' she cut in, 'not marriage. I don't mean that James. In her last letter she said that he's more like a son to her, that he was so thoughtful and she'd grown quite fond of him already. She said he was such good company for her. Even told me how they spent their evenings. Also that a girl friend of his is often a guest at the house on many weekends. I haven't thought of him as a threat until now — this letter. It's quite possible that if she grows too fond of him she might consider leaving the house to him. She's well aware that I would only sell it, that I'd never live permanently in England. The old place and the estate would be worth a lot of money.'

James Maddison handed back the letter then tossed off his drink. Looking thoughtful he went to pour another. 'Well honey I guess it's about time you took a vacation and paid the old girl a visit. I mean — let's face it — she's getting on and already had one stroke. An illness like this could bring on another and see her off at any time. She says herself in the letter if you leave it too long you may be too late. I suggest you go immediately honey or you may find yourself out of favour and cut off from any inheritance.' He finished his drink hastily and glanced at his watch. 'I'll have to go or Cora will accuse me of all-hell. We'll talk about this tomorrow at the office first thing. So long honey.' He kissed her hurriedly and left the apartment, and Paula Carpenter pondering over the letter.

★ ★ ★

In the high-rise block that housed the suite of Maddison Enterprises a man entered an office. After a cursory glance around he approached the desk where a typist was winding a sheet of quarto into a Remington. 'Thank you Miss Carpenter.' He placed a sheaf of papers down close to her on the desk top.

The girl smiled. 'I'm not Miss Carpenter. Don't worry though this is her desk and she'll be back at any moment.'

The man now on his way to the door turned back. 'I beg your pardon. I'm new here. I met Miss Carpenter for the first time only this morning and I thought — I mean you look so much like . . .'

'It's okay. You're not the only person I assure you. We're always being mistaken for each other. I'm Sally Lane. Here's Paula now.'

Paula Carpenter entered the office with James Maddison. The man regarded the faces of the two girls in turn and remarked, 'My you really do look alike — you could be sisters and I really mean that.'

As the door closed behind him Sally Lane looked amused and said. 'Would he believe half-sisters!'

Before she resumed her work at the typewriter she glanced at Paula Carpenter. 'Gee you sure could use a face lift right now. Where's the funeral!'

Paula seated herself at another desk to wait for Sally Lane to finish typing out a letter and commented huffily, 'How much longer are they going to take to repair yours?'

'Not long now. I thought you wouldn't mind my using yours once more while you were out of the office. I want to get this off in the next mail honey.'

'Well I'm back now.'

'Okay — okay.' Sally Lane whisked the paper from the typewriter. 'All finished. Say — what's bothering you! You two had a quarrel or something?'

'No. It's my aunt. On again for me to visit her. I can't put it off much longer. She's ill again. And I don't want to leave New York right now. I'm far too busy. Quite apart from the fact that I don't fancy the idea of burying myself in the English countryside.'

'Gee you must be crazy! Give me the chance and see if I'd say no!' Sally Lane rose to vacate the seat at the desk but promptly sat down again as James Maddison suddenly exclaimed. 'Say — that's it! Why not go in Paula's place? She hasn't seen the old girl for years which means the old girl hasn't seen her either. You both look so much alike. You heard what that guy just said.'

Sally Lane had opened her mouth a couple of times to speak but astonishment had stopped the words. A moment later she succeeded. 'Are you crazy! You must be! It's just not possible! I couldn't! They'd know. I don't speak the way Paula does. She has an

97

English touch in her voice because her mother was English. They'd remember. I'd give myself away!'

'Accents change. Besides Paula would sound all American to English ears.' James Maddison persisted with the idea which he thought was a brilliant one. 'You just claimed that given the chance you'd go. Well here it is. There is nothing to prevent you. Think of Paula. She could be disinherited in favour of this guy who's moved in with the old girl. Most probably he's already got designs on the property and whatever else is going.'

'But it would be deceitful! Dishonest! I really couldn't do it.'

'Why?' he counteracted. 'What harm could it do? In fact quite the reverse. It would make the old girl happy.'

Paula Carpenter who had also been momentarily stunned by the unexpected suggestion suddenly came to life. With a burst of enthusiasm she stood up and paced about the office as she spoke. 'It's a fantastic idea! You know how much you've always wanted to visit London. Redcliffe where my aunt lives is not so very far from there. It would be a free holiday for you. I'd pay the fare of course and all your expenses.' She paused to smile briefly before adding. 'Actually my aunt even offered to pay for my flight ticket. But of course I don't need that.'

Still bemused Sally Lane shook her head slowly. 'It's impossible Paula. I know nothing about your aunt or your past — or the house and the things you did there when you last visited. Your aunt would be sure to ask questions that I couldn't answer; especially about your mother. Strangers might mistake us for each other but your aunt would know the difference instantly.'

'I told you — my aunt hasn't seen me since I was 12 years old. That's eleven years ago. She has no photographs of me taken after that time. I've changed a whole lot since then. And I can tell you all you'd need to know about that visit and about the house and Redcliffe. At least all I remember myself. My aunt wouldn't expect me to recall every detail from so long ago. If she did mention something that I've forgotten to tell you about you have only to say that you don't recall. It's simple. And you'd have some young company there with her Mr Baines. He'd probably offer to show you around London. According to my aunt he is very good looking. At the same time you could weigh up what exactly his motives are in being there.'

By now Paula Carpenter was completely

stimulated by the idea and the possibility of dealing with the long promised visit to her aunt without leaving New York herself. Her enthusiasm began to communicate itself to Sally Lane who gave a nervous laugh of anticipation. She began to consider the prospect now they had made it appear simple. Then her face clouded. 'Passport. You're forgetting that. You see — it's impossible. What if the plane was delayed and she enquired whether you had caught the flight. She's bound to send someone to meet you at the airport and your name wouldn't be on the flight list.'

'My name *would* be on the passenger list. You can travel on my passport. No problem. Who's to know? We look enough alike. You know how bad passport photos are anyway.'

'That's right,' James Maddison pursued. 'How can anyone find out unless you tell them. I was struck by your resemblance to Paula when she first brought you here looking for a job.' He hoped this reminder of past favours might make her feel obliged. He was well aware that Paula, as the only relative, would inherit the English estate of her aunt. He and Paula had often discussed it, and he'd always intended to ensure that a cut of it came his way. The business needed some financial propping up and the sooner the better. At present his wife Cora held the purse strings and of late was threatening to pull out of the business altogether. It was necessary to cut himself free of her. Too long he'd been saddled to her crazy jealous whining when he was going out for the evening. There was a very good case for Sally Lane making a visit in Paula's place. If Paula went there was always the chance she might decide to stay, especially with the Baines guy there. She could get sweet on him. After all, the old lady apparently had. Paula was too financially valuable to the future of Maddison Enterprises. He didn't want to risk losing her. Until now the English inheritance had seemed assured regardless of whether or not she made the visit to her aunt. Now that confidence was undermined.

Intently the two waited for Sally Lane to acquiesce.

For Paula it would solve more than to ensure the continuing favour of her aunt. It would also mean that she need not leave New York and James Maddison, who in her absence would console himself with any girl interested in having a good time no expense spared. There would be many ready to jump at the opportunity of being wined and dined by a supposedly wealthy escort. Men such as he needed constant distractions from the irksome realities and pressures of large scale business concerns. A year ago he had been asking his wife for a divorce; but now he had reconciled himself with the fact that she did not intend to oblige. Only for the sake of the business did he stay with her. If he left her he knew that she'd turn vindictive and Maddison Enterprises couldn't afford that. Not that Paula Carpenter would have married him in any case. She didn't give much for the chances of wives of such men as he; although she had never actually told him this. Not that she entirely blamed these men. She had met a few of their wives; some seemed obsessed with petty social upstaging. Terrible boors she found them. Although Cora Maddison could not be pigeon-holed into this social slot of society. She was just a pathetic clinging vine who had turned into an alcoholic.

Paula did not want to leave the field open. She was infatuated with James Maddison; his dominant character appealed to her. It matched her own.

'Say you'll do it Sally,' she urged. 'You'd be doing me a great favour hun.'

Sally Lane got up from her chair and paced the office. She could think more clearly on the move. The prospect of a free trip to England was greatly tempting. She'd have the benefit of both worlds. To see London — her long time dream — and stay in the wonderful English countryside in a lovely country house the image of which she had only seen in travel brochures and books. At heart she was not a city person. Often she had yearned to be away from the noise and the crowds. Would it really be possible to pull off such a trick. Was it feasible that she would be taken at face value by Paula's aunt? The uncertainty made her head spin.

'Think of the holiday.' James Maddison pressed. 'Take a couple of months off. Longer if you like. You'll get paid so don't worry on that score.' His attention was distracted by a short fat man who opened the door and called, 'Hey Mad can you spare a few minutes in my office? I've got a problem.'

James Maddison held his arm up in acknowledgment and as he followed the man out called back, 'Ring up and book a table for three at Maxi's and we'll talk about it over lunch.'

As he left the office Sally Lane looked seriously thoughtful. Mad was the right name for him, coming up with such a wild idea! She'd be mad herself to get carried away with it.

Nevertheless lunch at Maxi's bore fruit for James Maddison and Paula Carpenter.

'If my cover gets blown you'd better be

ready to do some explaining to your aunt. I know I should not be able to handle that,' Sally Lane declared.

Paula gave her a quick hug. 'Thanks honey. I'm real grateful. Relax now everything will be just fine.'

Sally Lane prayed sincerely that it would be. In an attempt to conquer her qualms she fixed her thoughts on the lighter side. The holiday. Seeing England.

Because Paula had practically begged her to take her place she had found it hard to say no. She owed her a big favour really. Paula had been responsible for getting her the excellent and well-paid job that she held at Maddison Enterprises. Such an opportunity would never have normally come her way, especially as she had not really been qualified for the position at that time.

They had met each other for the very first time just after the motor accident that had claimed the lives of her mother and Paula's father. It was then that they discovered they'd been fathered by the same man. They had also learned that he and Sally's mother had known each other for 26 years. For reasons known only to themselves they had parted and many years passed before they had met again. By which time the man, whom Sally Lane had known as her father had died. Only after his death had the old association resumed. They had been reunited for only two years before the fatal car crash that had claimed both their lives.

7

Lydie plumped up the pillows on Emily Penne's bed, then stood back smiling. 'Comfortable?'

'Yes thank you Lydie dear. You know you shouldn't be spending your day off with a sick old woman. You get quite enough of that at the hospital. I told Charlie to take you out somewhere so that you could both enjoy a few hours off. Such a pity Clive can't get home this weekend. He'd not need any coaxing to whisk you off somewhere nice.'

'I wouldn't have gone. I'd rather be here than anywhere. I enjoy the peace and quiet of the country. And Charlie wouldn't go off and leave you when you're not well. I can't tell you how much I look forward to the weekends here in this lovely house.'

'I'm so glad Lydie. You know you're always more than welcome. I consider myself very fortunate to have met you and Charlie.' Emily Penne had fallen into the habit now of using the name Charlie, since Lydie always did and so did Clive. 'Having you both here makes me realise more than ever just how much William and I missed in having no children.

We always regretted the fact. But it was God's will so no reproaches to either of us. Now you must be very tired after being on night duty at the hospital. If you feel like having a nap go ahead. I want you to always treat this house as your own home.'

'Thank you. I shall. I do.' She bent to kiss Emily Penne on the cheek. 'But right now I'm going to sit here and read to you. Now where will I find this latest novel which Charlie bought for you?'

'On the bureau — if you're sure you wouldn't rather sleep. Where is Charlie? Still picking quinces?'

'I believe so. He should be just about finished now. I know Martha's waiting on them. What does she make? Jam or jelly?'

'Jelly. She makes it every year.'

Lydie settled herself on a small chaise longue covered in cherry velvet now faded with time. She slipped off her indoor shoes and sank her stockinged feet into the thick soft carpet. Opening the book at the place marked by a leather bookmark she proceeded to read. Ten minutes later when she glanced up she saw that Emily Penne had dozed off.

★ ★ ★

From a high shelf in the pantry Martha Oakes took down the last of the empty preserving jars. Then from the top-most shelf arranged some full jars of this season's raspberries closer together to make room for the quince jelly later. Some over-spill of syrup had caused one jar to stick to the newspaper with which she had lined the shelves the previous year. As she slid the jar aside the paper tore. With a mutter of annoyance she moved the jars to a lower shelf in order to reline the top one and something in the newspaper caught her eye. She held her breath, then released it in a viperish hiss. The constant nagging at her memory since the arrival of Charlie ended. Tense with victory and clutching the paper she stepped down from the chair. She spread the torn sheet out on the kitchen table to study a photograph and the printed words that accompanied it. Despite the beard she was certain that the man pictured was Charlie Baines. The name printed was Barnes but it was him all right, she'd swear to it. The newspaper was dated the previous year.

On several occasions when she'd stood on the chair to take down a jar of preserves the photograph had attracted her attention. Then by chance it had been covered by another full jar. As her eyes scanned the print a malicious expression of victory and power gradually spread to her sullen features. This should put paid to the schemes of Charlie Barnes. Even lied about his name. Emily Penne couldn't keep him on when she saw this proof. The girl would have to leave too. Couldn't pretend she didn't know. Muttering to herself she tore out the damning evidence with shaking hands. 'Breaking and entering! Burglary eh! Let's see what her ladyship has to say about that. Serves the stupid old fool right.' With the cutting clutched in her hand and a determined expression on her face she left the kitchen, totally ignoring Lydie who was about to enter.

At this same moment Charlie carrying a cardboard box containing newly picked quinces entered the kitchen by the back door that led off from the orchard. He put the box down on the floor and greeted Lydie with a broad smile. 'Hello nurse, how's the patient this morning?'

'Much better. Dozed off while I was reading to her. I think she should get up tomorrow. Not good for her to stay in bed for too long. She needs to exercise her left side or she could lose the use of it altogether.'

'And where's old sourpuss — ?' Charlie broke off as he caught sight of the newspaper on the table with the tell-tale piece ripped out. Almost word for word he could have quoted the articles of news that had surrounded the picture. Often he'd read it. He had retained it specially for the purpose of asking a few of his fellow inmates at the prison if they thought he would be recognised from the photograph. That was after having shaved off the beard that he'd worn at the time of the photograph. Answering opinions had varied.

'People don't hang on to newspaper pictures of petty crims even if they do look like bloody film stars.'

And . . . 'You shouldn't go in for crime with a phiziog like yours. People are bound to remember.'

These had not been definite enough answers, so he still had never been sure. Lydie couldn't tell him because she was too accustomed to his face with and without the beard. Now he was confronted with the answer to that old question. Many times he had cursed himself for not noticing the damned newspaper photographer at the courts that day. As a rule they didn't bother with the likes of petty offenders unless a celebrity or well-known identity. His notice-able looks had worked against him that time.

In one stride he reached the table and snatched up the now torn page of newsprint.

'Where the devil did she — ?' He saw the dark red fruit stain which provided the answer. His carefree manner of the moment before vanished along with his hopes for a decent future as he thought of the damning evidence in the palm of Martha Oakes spiteful hands. He threw a cursory glance to the open pantry door. 'This must have been on the shelf all along! Where is she?'

Instantly Lydie understood what had happened. 'She just passed me.' Lydie hadn't kept the news report herself but a glance now at the date on the paper was enough; *that* she remembered well. Many nights during those first weeks that followed she had cried herself to sleep at the thought of Charlie in that awful place. She had been shocked and disappointed in him and the reason for his being there. Abruptly she turned and hurried from the room.

Charlie slowly followed into the hall and watched her as she ran up the stairs. An air of dejection settled over him and he sank down onto the lower stairs. He rested his elbows on his knees and his head in his hands. What bothered him most of all was the thought of the old lady's disillusionment. He genuinely cared very much about her personal opinion of him. He had tried to live up to the image he had drawn for himself since coming to

Grandstone House. He had become very attached to her, and so had Lydie. Well, at least he'd done no harm. Quite the reverse. They'd brightened up her life. She'd said so herself, quite often. He lifted his head suddenly as he considered the effect this would have on Lydie who had not set out to deceive as he had. It would mean the end of her association with Clive Wessley; in addition to the embarrassment that would be inflicted on her. He silently cursed meddlesome Martha Oakes.

With all this in mind he wondered if it were possible to deny that the photograph was of himself; bluff his way out by claiming that any resemblance was purely coincidental. It would of course be simple enough for Emily Penne to check on this. Yet he felt confident that she would not.

He wondered what Lydie had in mind rushing off upstairs like that. No doubt an attempt to prevent the venomous old cat of a housekeeper from exposing him. Little hope of that. Lydie had shown courage in going up without hesitation — to fly in the face of confrontation. And he'd not had the grace to follow and support her. Suddenly he stood up and sprinted up the stairs. He could at least speak up for her loyalty to him, and for her innocence with regard to his past sins.

The door to Emily Penne's room was partly open. He was about to knock and enter when through the hinge-side gap he caught sight of Martha Oakes holding out the cutting for inspection. She had obviously dropped her bombshell already.

Charlie let his hand fall away without contacting the door. He watched Lydie straightening the bed-covers. In an attempt to delay the moment of truth she was remarking inanely — 'You were asleep when I left you a few moments ago,' as if her pointless words might have some miraculous effect in preventing Emily from studying the photograph. At the same time she shot an accusing look at the housekeeper who merely returned a hostile expression while awaiting the expected reaction.

Emily Penne reached for her spectacles to study the photograph.

With breath held and trying to give an impression of unconcern Lydie occupied herself in tidying various objects in the room. She was ready to scornfully deny seeing any resemblance.

Time stood suspended while the verdict was awaited. For an eternity it seemed the old lady held the cutting before her. Then with a sudden movement and showing off-hand disinterest she handed the cutting back. 'Why

Martha you're getting fanciful in your old age!' Then she waved her right hand in an unmistakable gesture of dismissal.

An expression of pure disbelief showed on the face of Martha Oakes, along with a flush of furious indignation. With a venomous glare at Lydie she swept out of the room.

As she went Emily Penne added — 'Will you set the table for three please Martha, four if you'll join us yourself. I suddenly feel a lot better and will come down to lunch.' Then she smiled, and Lydie who had flopped down onto the chaise in relief stood up again and on a sudden impulse went across to hug her. 'I'm so glad you're feeling better.' Tears pricked her eyes and she smiled to blink them away; for she strongly suspected that Emily Penne had seen what Martha had intended her to see.

'Now what about another chapter from that book. I promise I shan't fall asleep halfway through this time. Then I shall dress and go downstairs.'

Outside the room Charlie had just enough time to dart across to his own room before Martha Oakes stalked out, her movements taut and bristling.

She returned to the kitchen and proceeded to reline the pantry shelves with fresh paper. Every movement of her body was driven by resentment at having been treated like an idiot. She had at least expected a showdown and the dismissal of Charlie so-called Baines. Instead she had received only a rebuff from the old fool who obviously didn't want to see the truth even when shoved right under her nose. Didn't *want* to because it would mean losing all the attention, all the spoiling. Oh no that must continue at all costs, regardless of his being an impostor as well as an ex-jailbird who would undoubtedly have made off with the valuables long ago if he were not after bigger fish. As she stepped down from the chair she glared at the box of quinces with distaste since the harvesting was the result of his labours.

With an angry action she snatched off her apron — the jelly could damn well wait. There was now a more urgent matter to attend to. She strode across the hall and upstairs. On the way to her bedroom to change her shoes she glanced through the open doorway of Emily Penne's room and saw that she was lying back eyes closed, a faint smile on her face. Lydie, on the small chaise, had fallen asleep over the book that looked as if it was about to slide from her knees to the floor. 'Make the most of things young miss,' she muttered as she passed, 'this'll be your last visit here. The old fool will

115

have to believe it the next time she's told.'

After witnessing Emily's dismissal of the housekeeper and the damning news-cutting Charlie, still marvelling at his narrow escape, returned to the orchard to collect the ladder and return it to the garage. As he came round the side of the house he saw the black-coated figure of Martha Oakes riding off on the old upright. He wondered at her change of plans about making the jelly after all the preparation with the jars. Something in her manner and expression made him uneasy. He hurried into the house to wash his hands in the downstairs cloakroom. Not stopping to change his clothes he collected the car keys, returned to the garage and drove the car out.

Having allowed enough time for her to reach the village he followed, certain that she had something not to his advantage in mind, and he could make a fair guess what it was.

In the village main street his eyes sought out the old upright. It was not outside any of the shops. He drove up a side street and saw it resting against the kerb outside the village police station. His unlit pipe held tightly between clenched teeth he headed back to Grandstone House.

Emily Penne had once mentioned that she had known the local police sergeant for many years. As an old acquaintance, perhaps even friend, he would have her interests at heart. He would also have known Martha Oakes a very long time and she would find a willing and receptive ear. He would be obliged to check up and was in a position to do so.

'Old besom's got me this time,' he muttered as he garaged the car on his return.

For a while he sat fingering the steering wheel, certain that this time there could be no reprieve.

Ten minutes later Lydie found him in his room standing at the window which over-looked the front gardens and driveway. His door was standing wide open and as she entered he turned. For the first time in her memory he gave no answering smile when she greeted him. 'Charlie, it's all right. Emily — '

'I know,' Charlie cut in.

'Charlie you should have seen Martha's face!' Lydie gave a light giggle.

'I did.'

'You did? Then why so glum?'

'The old cat's gone to the police.'

Lydie's smile faded. 'How do you know that?'

'I followed her into the village.'

Lydie shrugged. 'Well so what? You haven't done anything illegal. You haven't committed any crime in coming here to work. What if he does check. I honestly don't think it will bother Emily now because I feel sure she already knows, thanks to meddlesome Martha.'

'It'll bother me — her knowing.'

'But she knows that you haven't done anything wrong since you've been working for her. You haven't attempted to rob or cheat her.' She paused briefly to search his eyes before adding. 'You haven't have you Charlie?'

He looked surprised and hurt at the question. 'Of course not Lyd. Not that I haven't had the opportunity. She signs all the cheques before I've even made them out when I do the accounts. And she'd be none the wiser. She doesn't even check the bank statements when they arrive. Everything of that nature has been assigned to me. She trusts me completely. I'd never betray that trust Lyd. You must know that. I could never bring myself to cheat her even if I was tempted — which I'm not. I know when I'm well off. Or at least I did.' He turned back to look out of the window. 'I've really grown to enjoy the work out there. Gardening gets to you; apart from which I've really grown fond of the old girl. She's not arrogant and bent on preserving the distinction between employer and worker. Not at all snobby. An unusual lady.'

'And a real one,' Lydie agreed readily. 'My

mother once said that you can always tell a real lady because a real lady is never a snob.'

Charlie smiled now and with a touch of irony said, 'But one can't always tell a real gentleman by all accounts.' He turned away from the window. 'I'm going to pack my things. I can't face her after taking her in the way I did. I shall leave a note for her though — to put you in the clear. I don't want to spoil things between you and Wessley. I'll say that you lost touch with me for a year or so and knew nothing of what I did during that time. Remember to appear surprised at the news. Our Ron'll be disappointed too. I wrote to him yesterday to tell him that we'd pick him up at the station on Saturday and take him to a show. I was sure that by then Emily would have recovered. I'll post another letter off to him today. Perhaps you can drive her to church this Sunday morning Lyd. You'll stay on. She'll have nothing against you when she reads my note.'

'She won't be up to attending church this week after a fortnight in bed. But we'll see. And Charlie . . . ' she held out her hand to delay him as he turned to leave the room to fetch his case from the boxroom, 'Please don't go unless you really have to. Stay and face her. You can't be positive that Martha went to the police for that purpose. And even if she did it may not do her any good. I told you that I'm certain Emily dismissed the news cutting purposely. Don't run away Charlie. I've never known you be a coward before.'

At the door now he turned back to face her. She had won her point even if over a doubt-ridden surrender. He smiled his old smile and took her by the hand. 'Are you telling me to stay and shoot it out with Martha Oakes?'

She nodded. 'And I'm saying don't go until Emily tells you to — because I'm sure she never will Charlie. Go on as before. Let her be the one to mention it if she wishes. I'm convinced that she won't. Least said soonest mended — as the old saying goes.'

'Come on then,' he decided. 'Lets go and see if she's awake.'

As Lydie had predicted Emily Penne did not mention Martha Oakes and the newspaper cutting. On Sunday morning she announced that she was well enough to attend the church service since it was from door to door. Lydie went with them.

Clive Wessley was unable to get away for this weekend as a major crime was under investigation. To quote him . . . 'All hands are required on deck.' Instead he had arranged to see Lydie one evening during the week when she was off duty.

Behind the curtain Martha Oakes watched them drive off in the Bentley. When it was out of view she hurried upstairs to the bedroom that had become Lydie's for her weekend stays. Not quite knowing what she expected to find she cast her eyes about the room. An overnight bag was placed on the floor beside the wardrobe. She was aware that Lydie lived in at the nurse's quarters and might well have to share accommodation with others. She deduced that personal papers, for privacy reasons, would be packed and carried when away overnight. The bag had been emptied of its contents such as would be required for a weekend stay; nightdress, robe, hairbrush and toiletries. There were no personal papers. She searched the drawers of the dressing table and chest of drawers but found these contained little more than spare handker-chiefs and a couple of scarves. She glanced in the wardrobe. Only one or two garments hung there. Annoyed she was about to leave the room. On the way to the door she paused as she remembered something she had noticed earlier. Lydie had been carrying a light-coloured handbag when she'd left for church. Yet when she'd arrived on Saturday she had been carrying a black one. It had been left on the hall table for a short while when Lydie had gone into the downstairs cloakroom. That bag must be in the room somewhere. She opened the wardrobe again and pulled aside the after-five dress hanging there. This revealed a black handbag suspended by its strap on a coat hanger close to the dress that had concealed it. She snatched the bag from the hanger. On first inspection it appeared to be empty except for a neatly folded handkerchief. She pulled aside the elastic topped inner pouch and saw a letter. Snatching this out she opened it to read. No address was written on the top of the page; simply the name Charlie. As she read she muttered the words aloud. A note of triumph gradually entered her voice as she read.

Dear Lydie

Thanks for writing to me. Your letters are all I have to look forward to apart from leaving this place. I don't blame you for not wanting to visit me. I wouldn't want you to come here anyway. I know what a bloody fool I've been. I must have been out of my senses. I've got plans for when I come out though. Nothing that's not law-abiding I promise so don't worry. This is the first and last time I ever see the inside of a prison — believe me. I do a lot of reading to pass the time. I'm studying gardening books at present and finding them very interesting. I had a letter from Ron yesterday. He's a good kid. I told him to come to you if he needed anything. If he does you can give him the money for it, within reason of course, from the bag I left with you. Use your discretion. I hope your mum is better now. Keep writing to me Lyd. Yours Charlie.

A short poem followed but Martha was too tense with success to bother to read it. It followed a postscript and was signed by its author Charlie Barnes.

She replaced the letter in its envelope and sat down on the bed to think. In her hands she held the proof about Charlie so-called Baines. But she could not show it to anyone without having to admit how she had come by it. However incriminating, Emily Penne would never tolerate the prying into her guest's private belongings. She wondered why there was only the one letter. He must have written more. Perhaps this one had been kept on account of the poem.

Still smarting from dismissal and being called fanciful she replaced the letter in the bag and returned this to the wardrobe. She could not even show the letter to George Hill without telling him how it came to be in her possession. Yet it would take this evidence to convince him. Silly old fool hadn't taken it seriously when she'd shown him the newspaper cutting. Full of excuses not to do anything about it. As good as said it wasn't any of his business. She recalled his exact words . . . 'Even if it is him I've no cause to go interfering. He's obviously been satisfactorily employed with Emily for the last six months or so and she must be quite happy with the way he's doing the work or she wouldn't have kept him on. As for the story about living abroad — well — it's commonly used as a reason to explain lack of recent employment. I shouldn't think there's anything to be concerned about Martha. If anything untoward comes to my notice I'll have a word with Emily.'

Martha considered she had been fobbed off.

★ ★ ★

On the following Saturday John and Mary Wessley came to Grandstone House to dine. This weekend Clive could not get home. Instead he had collected Lydie from the hospital on Wednesday for an evening out.

Lydie was on her usual weekend visit and at the insistence of Emily Penne had gone into town for the evening with Charlie.

'You've both been staying in too much at weekends just lately on my account. In any case I shall have company for the evening so shan't be alone,' she'd assured them.

During the evening she requested the Wessleys to each witness her signature on a document that she had by phone instructed her family solicitor to prepare. The document had been delivered to Grandstone House by registered mail and she had dealt with it personally since she did not want Charlie to see it.

After sealing it, along with a letter which she'd written earlier, she put it on the hall table for him to post by registered mail on Monday morning.

★ ★ ★

Emily Penne smiled to herself as she made her way downstairs wearing her old fur coat. Charlie had told her to wrap up well against the cool October breeze.

This would be her first walk in the garden since being confined to bed. After church on Sunday the weather had turned damp and he had insisted that she stay in the house. How like William he was with his thoughtful concern for her. During the past two weeks she had missed their garden strolls.

125

As she was making her way across the hall towards the sewing room the telephone rang. She retraced her steps to answer. 'Emily Penne speaking.'

When the caller announced himself she responded in surprise. 'Oh good morning George. How are you keeping?' As she listened in silence while Sergeant George Hill at the local police station stated his reason for the call a small frown appeared on her brow. Then she responded. 'I appreciate your concern for me George but I do assure you that it is quite unnecessary to make inquiries regarding Mr Baines. I know all I need to know thank you. Martha is a fanciful busybody. Don't pander to her.' She paused briefly to listen again, then continued. 'Yes I know that, but coincidences often defy credibility. Remember that George. Now you must drop in for a drink some time.' She replaced the receiver and resumed her way out through the French door into the garden, a flush of anger colouring her pale cheeks; yet a spark of humour in her eyes.

Unnoticed Martha Oakes at a corner off the hall stepped back into the laundry room and collected up a bowl of washing. Through a side door she went into the garden where autumn sunlight fell in stark contrast on her glowering face.

8

On his way to morning tea with Emily Penne Charlie gathered up the mail from the floor just inside the front door. A blue and red stripe edged envelope made a bright splash of colour among the other letters. Unnecessarily he glanced at the address of the sender. A small frown puckered his brow, but disappeared the instant he reached the doorway of the drawing room.

Smiling he held up the brightly bordered envelope as he entered the room. 'Oh Charlie!' Emily Penne smiled broadly showing her delight. 'Open it at once please and read it out to me.'

Charlie seated himself and obliged.

Dear Aunt Emily

I hope by now you have recovered from your chill and are up and about again. I had to delay my reply to your last letter in order to give myself time to make plans for my much postponed visit to you. I can now give you a definite date for my arrival. Everything is arranged for the flight and I shall be arriving on November 5th which means that I'll be able to spend Christmas with you. I am looking forward to seeing you and the old house again. I shall telephone nearer the day to let you know the expected time of my arrival at the airport so that you can arrange for your man to collect me. I'll keep this letter brief since I shall be seeing you very shortly. Your loving niece Paula.

When Charlie looked up from the letter he saw that she was clasping her hands together in delight and smiling broadly.

'After all these years my only living relative has decided to pay me a visit. That letter you wrote for me brought luck Charlie. I do hope she doesn't fall in love with you, although I'm sure she will, and entice you back to America with her. I feel absolutely certain she'll never settle here in England. At least — not unless her ideas have very much changed.'

Charlie forced a light laugh. 'No worries about that. I'll never leave Grandstone House unless you throw me out.'

She looked pleased. 'And no worries about that either for I shall never do that.' She smiled fondly and in a more serious tone added, 'I promise you.'

9

NEW YORK

Sally Lane swept a last brief glance around the small apartment as she heard the cab driver announce his arrival with a quick toot on the horn. Uncertain how long she would be away on the overseas visit she had given up the lease. When she returned from England she would stay with Paula until new accommodation was found. The belongings that she would be leaving behind her had already been collected by James Maddison to store at Paula's apartment.

Although nervous she was looking forward to her trip and her stay at the English country house. It had all been made to appear so straightforward and simple. Constantly, since agreeing to the madcap idea, she recalled their encouraging words to mind. This boosted her confidence when at times it flagged.

She picked up the two suitcases and clicked the lock on the door behind her. The cab driver appeared and took the cases from her. On arrival at Paula's apartment she paid and dismissed him.

Arrangements had been made for Paula to drive her to the airport terminal and see her off. She settled down to wait the ten minutes still to go until the planned time for Paula to arrive. A quarter of an hour passed. She telephoned the office to check that Paula had left and was assured that she had. Concerned about the fast approaching flight time she paced the apartment, anxious to be gone. If she left it any longer she would miss the plane.

From the coffee table she picked up an envelope that contained Paula's birth certificate and passport and put it in her bag. As she reached for the telephone to order a cab it rang. Nerves tense now she snatched up the receiver. 'Oh Paula — thank heaven! What hap . . . '

'Trouble with the car honey. I'm afraid I'll never make it. I'm stuck at . . . in a call box at . . . highway.'

The sound of heavy traffic passing in the background drowned some of the words.

'I don't know exactly where James is right this minute so can't contact him to ask him to collect you and drive you to the airport. He had to attend an important conference. I guess he'd be too far away in any case to make it to the apartment on time. So sorry not to be there to see you off hun. Don't wait any longer. Call a cab. Don't go without the passport . . . ' her words were momentarily drowned again by the sound of heavy traffic. 'Now relax and don't worry about a thing. All will be okay I just know it. Have a good trip and enjoy the holiday. Wait until you're properly settled before you write to me. And remember not to let anyone see you address the envelope in my name. Have to watch those little things. Bye hun. Take — ' Her words were drowned again by background noise. The phone went dead and Sally Lane felt suddenly cut off and alone. She had relied on Paula being with her until the last moment to sustain her courage and confidence until she boarded the aircraft. As she replaced the receiver she glanced across at her luggage standing by the door. Then across to the bags and suitcases that contained her belongings to be left behind with Paula. She felt that she was losing her own identity; it was packed there in those bags, boxes and cases, estranged from her life for the present.

With trembling fingers she dialled for another taxicab, wishing that she'd not dismissed the last one.

10

NEW YORK

In the courtyard of the apartment block Cora Maddison parked her yellow coupe and switched off the engine. Her eyes searched along the row of vehicles already standing there. With surprise she noted that the blue convertible which belonged to Paula Carpenter was not among them. She had phoned the offices of Maddison Enterprises and been told that Miss Carpenter had already left the building. She now scanned the windows on the fifth floor. Some were already lit up.

Having checked, she was aware that her husband was indeed attending a board meeting. A genuine one this time, not just an excuse to be late home as had been the case countless times over the past few years, and in particular the last two. She was also aware that he would call here at Paula Carpenter's apartment when he left the meeting. But it would be for the last time.

She leaned across and opened the flap of the glove compartment, which revealed a small hand gun and a bottle half full of gin.

She reached for the bottle, removed the stopper and drank. All the while she watched for the blue convertible. Fifteen minutes later she idly inspected the empty bottle and let it slide through her fingers to the floor of the car. Again she reached over and took out the gun and put it in the pocket of her coat. While she watched and waited her fingers drummed impatiently on the steering wheel.

For her the final straw which had tipped the precarious tension scales had come yesterday when he'd forgotten her birthday. While she'd been out at the stores he had left a telephone message with the cleaning woman to say that he'd be home late. Always he made it appear unavoidable; as if some urgent matter had come up unexpectedly at the offices.

Repeatedly over the years he'd had fleeting affairs with various women. For eleven long years she had tolerated the situation because none had lasted any length of time. Until this last one. For Paula Carpenter he had requested a divorce. True he hadn't pressed the matter too hard when she'd refused. Perhaps he had only asked to satisfy the girl.

Money was and always had been his prime concern. She wished afterwards that she had called his bluff about the divorce. He knew which side his bread was buttered.

133

If their marriage had produced children she might more easily have endured his off-hand treatment of her; or at least resigned herself to it, because she would have had someone to share the long lonely hours with. Instead she had turned to drink for consolation. Well, now she wanted out. She'd had enough of the life that had been disillusionment for most of those eleven years. One thing was certain — he would get one hell of a surprise when he discovered the alteration she had made in her will. All to charity — a children's home where it would be put to good use. Knowing this gave her the satisfaction of doing something worthwhile in her life and a feeling of redemption.

She gave a low humorous laugh and her head drooped forward onto her arms resting across the steering wheel. It was almost dusk now. She raised her head at the sound of a car driving into the courtyard. Vacantly she glanced at the taxicab and was about to lower her head once more when she saw the passenger get out and pay the driver. Cora Maddison was alert now and she wondered vaguely why Paula Carpenter was not using her blue convertible. Cora knew the car, having previously followed her home from the offices one day a few weeks ago, and parked at a discreet distance she had then seen her husband arrive and enter the apartment block.

The light from an overhead lamp fell onto Paula Carpenter as she went in the main door. Cora, tense and alert now, waited for the light to go on in a window on the fifth floor. Unsteadily now she got from the car. Moments later she entered the building. She knew which apartment to head for having made it her business one afternoon to find out. As she made her way there now her hand closed over the gun in her pocket. Her other hand strayed to another pocket and closed round a small bottle of pills.

High volume sounds from a television could be heard clearly. The time slot was for young viewing and a cowboy western film was in its final minutes. Someone opened a door and the noise of gunfire rushed out to her ears. A sudden flash of clear thought penetrated briefly through her befuddled mind. She wondered where the point was in killing the girl and then taking her own life. It was *he* who should die, as he deserved. This way nothing would change for him. He would go on in the same old way, except that he would lose Maddison Enterprises. That would hit him where it most hurt. It wouldn't take him long to find another woman; especially one with money. That was all he had married her for. She knew him so well by now. Enough even to know that when he found the girl's body he would flee the apartment. She doubted that he'd even stop to call the police. His own neck would take priority. A bitter half smile twisted her lips as she imagined him speeding home as if the devil were on his tail. 'Enough is enough,' she muttered, as her mind in its present state lost touch with reality. 'I'll kill the bastard too.' When he came home tonight she would be waiting with the gun.

She had reached the apartment now and discovered the door ajar. The name on it danced briefly before her glazed eyes then settled back to readable order. A television close by sent out a loud exploding sound of gunfire combined with action music as she slowly pushed open the door and stepped inside.

Paula Carpenter was bent over a television in the process of switching on and did not look up. The hand that raised the gun was steady now as Cora Maddison stepped forward.

As she pulled the trigger in unison with the wild west hero of the screen, squalling Indians made a hasty retreat on horseback and Paula Carpenter sank slowly to the floor.

* * *

James Maddison drummed his fingers on the driving wheel of his Cadillac and cursed aloud while he waited for the traffic lights to turn green. He was already running late. He had especially wanted to be at Paula's apartment in time to see Sally Lane off in case she had last minute second thoughts to be quashed. But the board meeting had dragged on and a lot had depended financially on his being there until the end. Cora was being difficult about investing more money and had been threatening to pull out of the company altogether. All out of spite. 'F . . . . . . cow,' he muttered.

The lights changed and the car sped forward. By now he guessed that Sally Lane would be at the air-terminal and wondered if it would be best to go straight there. He decided to check at the apartment first, just in case, to make certain she really had left.

As he drove into the courtyard of the apartment block he was shocked to see his wife drive off — the tyres of her yellow coupe screeching on the tarmac, and her eyes staring straight ahead. 'What the bloody hell!' he said aloud. How had she found out? And why the devil was she driving like a bloody mad-woman! Obviously been drinking as usual.

Automatically he glanced up at the window

on the fifth floor as he got from the car and hurried into the building.

*   *   *

The plane was airborne. Too late now to have doubts. Sally Lane tried to relax in her seat but the full significance of what she was doing suddenly thrust itself violently upon her. Now that she was alone the deceit upon which she had embarked was magnified. During its planning, with the three of them, it had seemed no more than a harmless adventure that would hurt nobody. Now doubt was uppermost in her thoughts. Responsible people did not go to such measures; not in real life. Such behaviour happened only in books.

The tiny apartment that she had so readily left behind her now seemed like a sanctuary to which she would have gladly fled had she not been high in the air looking down over the skyscrapers of pulsating New York City.

*   *   *

'Jesus!' James Maddison closed the door and leaned heavily against it as he stared in fascinated horror at the body of Paula Carpenter on the floor.

138

'Jesus!' he repeated. 'What's the bitch done!' He moved now and knelt beside the body to check the pulse. Slowly he got up and went across to the telephone. His hand hovered . . . an ambulance or doctor could be of no use now. He needed to think first. He was in one hell of a mess. Bloody insane bitch Cora! Jealous drunken cow!

He became aware of the television newscaster who had replaced the cowboy and strode across to switch off the set. A bloody drink first — that's what he needed. He went over to a small side-table where the bottles of drink and glasses were waiting and poured himself a large measure of whisky which he drank where he stood before pouring another. With this in his hand he paced the room and again cursed aloud. Bloody altered everything! His mind worked fast as he paced, drinking at intervals, while he decided what his next step must be. Alternately his eyes focused on the body on the floor and the telephone.

Cora Maddison had been correct in predicting that his first concern would be for himself. But, for two reasons, was wrong in supposing that he would flee the scene and run straight home to her waiting gun. How was she to know that in killing his mistress she had created for him a situation from which there was no immediate flight. Things were not that simple. And there was no waiting gun. Cora herself was dead; her body crushed in the mangled yellow coupe that she had swerved drunkenly into the path of an oncoming truck, just off of a main highway.

He glanced at his watch. Only five minutes had passed since he had entered the apartment. It seemed like an hour. He sank into an armchair his mind furiously active. He could now wave goodbye to the English inheritance and estate. His watch told him that the plane had now left. Yet there was always the possibility that it had been delayed. With this thought he jerked himself up from the chair and went to telephone. On the pad alongside this Paula had noted the flight number and departure time, also the airport number. He dialled and made the enquiry and was told, 'The flight left on schedule sir.'

Without thanks or acknowledgment he banged down the receiver with a loud curse. He would just have to catch her at the other end; leave a message for her to contact him on arrival at London airport before she was met by the Baines guy as arranged. He took another swig from the glass in his hand. As he drank he threw a cursory glance at the boxes and cases that contained the belongings of

Sally Lane; items from her apartment to be stored here to await her return. These were still in the spot where they had been left two days ago. He picked up the receiver to make the call to Heathrow to arrange for the message to be put out on arrival of her flight. As he waited for the connection his eyes again travelled to the cases and boxes on the floor a few feet away. This time his focus lingered and his expression changed. When a voice at the other end of the line spoke he replied absently, 'Never mind. Forget it.' While his hand slowly replaced the receiver his thoughts were racing in contrast to the movement. 'That's it!' he muttered. A solution. No need to stop Sally Lane. She could go ahead as planned. Who was to know if she made a permanent swap of identity with Paula. To aid his calculating thoughts he paced the room quickly now while he constructed a plan that would enable him to still get his hands on the English estate. Paula could be buried as Sally Lane. He would make the formal identification of the body since he was the one most qualified. He recalled Sally Lane once mentioning that she had no family connections apart from a very distant uncle living somewhere in Kentucky or Virginia, he couldn't remember that detail. He recalled what she had jokingly said — 'He is distant and distant.' He was sure also that she'd said she'd never even met him. In which case, if traced, he could not be called upon to make formal identification. There appeared to be no snags. Nobody but the three of them knew about the blood relationship between the two girls. The identity of the murderer was known. There was no mystery to the case. He would simply say that Sally Lane had arrived at the apartment to stay while Paula was overseas. He would have to insist that he must be the one to break the news to her on her arrival in England. He would tell the police that the shooting had been a case of mistaken identity. It shouldn't be hard to convince them, considering the state of Cora's mind and blood alcohol level. He knelt down to search the pockets of the jacket which Paula was wearing, in case there was something that might give away her identity. Having satisfied himself on this he went to search in her handbags. He found one and removed her driving licence. It contained nothing else that would suggest her to be other than Sally Lane. Suddenly remembering the car he went to check that it held nothing to indicate that she hadn't left New York.

Five minutes later he returned to the apartment puzzled at the absence of the blue convertible. On his arrival he hadn't noticed that it was missing, his wife's car had taken all his attention. But he didn't expect that the police would have any cause to enquire about the car. Fortunately Sally Lane did not own one.

He glanced at the telephone and decided against calling the police until he'd given some more thought to the situation. They'd ask what he was doing in the apartment if his mistress was on her way overseas. Tricky ground there. Briefly he considered telling them that he was having an affair with them both, then dismissed the idea. It would only complicate matters further. He'd tell them he had called at the apartment to check that Paula had caught the flight, because he'd been unable to get away in time to see her off; that he had arrived in time to see his wife driving off, and then had found the body.

His thoughts switched back to Sally Lane. He need not let her know about all this until she was actually settled at the country house. Then it would be too late for her to panic and run or do anything about it. She would be obliged to carry on the pretence. That way the inheritance could still be claimed, likely in the near future considering the state of the old lady's health and her age.

To satisfy himself that there was nothing to

belie the story that Paula had travelled overseas he checked over the apartment thoroughly.

Then with another quick glance at the body on the floor he picked up the phone.

11

Oblivious of the tragic drama which she'd left behind her Sally Lane settled back into the soft leather comfort of the Bentley. As Charlie turned the key in the ignition she tried to conceal her nervousness. The deception had begun. 'I thought I'd never recognise you from . . . ' she paused, 'from my aunt's description. I guess I imagined that all Englishmen would be wearing tweeds.' She recalled the exact words in the letter to Paula from her aunt — You'll recognise Charlie instantly. Just look for the handsomest young man around wearing tweeds and smoking a pipe. She had spotted him instantly.

Charlie smiled as he set the car in motion. 'I was about to put out a message asking you to come to the spot where I was waiting. Your aunt did show me a photograph but you were very much younger when it was taken and I don't think it would have helped very much.'

On the drive to Redcliffe she felt tense with the knowledge that she had to be on guard at all times in order not to give herself away. She had memorised the information which Paula had given to her about the country house and her last visit, along with what little family history Paula herself knew. It was very little to remember really. Paula had even mentioned the nearest neighbours to Grandstone House. She felt apprehensive about meeting Clive Wessley on account of his being a detective. She had voiced her qualms to Paula and been assured — 'Clive Wessley would never remember me. I have no recollection of what he looks like. He was a teenager back then.' Paula had laughed about the other fear. 'I can't think of him as any kind of policeman even though I don't recall his face. I vaguely remember that he was polite and even a little shy.'

When they reached the village of Redcliffe she wondered whether she should feign some pretence at recollection of the house at first sight when the time came. Yet didn't want to add unnecessarily to the deception if she could avoid it.

'Almost there now,' Charlie cast a quick glance at her. 'Nervous?' He could tell that she was. He hadn't expected that in someone from New York. Until this moment he hadn't asked any personal questions except about her flight. He had spoken only to remark on various places of special interest along the way.

'Why no,' she lied, knowing from his

question that it must be obvious that she was. Doubts were sapping her confidence. Surely they would all see that she was not Paula. In an attempt to charge her flagging courage she recalled the encouraging words of Paula and James Maddison. 'How can they possibly know unless you tell them?' She stole a quick glance at Charlie's handsome profile. The fact that he looked such a gentleman made her feel the weight of deceit and guilt more intensely. To her dismay she now found herself trembling slightly.

When Charlie had turned the corner into Berry Lane he turned briefly to look at her. The look extracted response.

'Just excited I guess — that's all.'

As he drove the Bentley through the big iron gates of Grandstone House she wondered again how she should respond. Perhaps she ought to show some small sign of recognition. Although she did not have to convince Charlie she reminded herself. He would have no cause to suspect her.

When he brought the car to a halt at the end of the long winding driveway she could barely conceal her surprise at the size of the house. It was much grander than she could ever have imagined. She wondered anew why on earth Paula had been so unwilling to come on a visit.

Charlie got out and opened the passenger door for her. He led the way up the steps to the front entrance and stood aside for her to enter first.

As she stepped into the vast hall she saw Emily Penniston-Barkley for the first time. Suddenly her knees felt too fragile for her own weight.

Smiling a warm welcome the old lady came forward her hands outstretched. 'Oh my dear Paula. How wonderful to see you again at long last. I've looked forward so much to this.' Affectionately she kissed the young cheek, then stood back a little to regard her visitor. 'I should never have known you. You were only a child when you were here last. Do you remember that visit?'

'The house is so much larger than I . . . ' Sally Lane broke off lamely, unwilling to lie with words just yet.

She was glad of a little distraction made by Charlie as he removed his top-coat and said, 'I'll go and fetch the luggage in from the car.'

'I hope you had a pleasant journey dear,' Emily Penne continued as she led her guest into the drawing room. 'I expect you're quite fatigued and ready for a meal. What do you think of the countryside so far?'

Sally Lane could at least answer this honestly. 'I think it's wonderful, so vastly

148

different from New York.

'I'm sure it must be. I'll get Charlie to take you for some long country drives. What did you think of him by the way? Handsome isn't he?'

'Yes — yes he is.' This also could be answered without deceit. 'I shall look forward to seeing more of the countryside.'

When Martha Oakes entered the room five minutes later Sally Lane was seated on the velvet covered chesterfield opposite Emily Penne who was in her usual wing-back chair.

'I expect you'll remember Martha. She hasn't changed very much over the last ten years or so. Although I must say you have Paula dear. You've certainly grown up very pretty.'

'Thank you.' Sally Lane acknowledged the compliment and smiled across at Martha Oakes. 'Nice to see you Martha.' She rose and was about to extend her hand, but the only response she received was a curt nod of the head which forestalled the hand gesture. Sally Lane wished that the woman would say something instead of staring at her in that aloof manner — as if she could see right through her.

'Will you show Paula up to her room Martha please. I'm sure she must want to freshen up after the long journey.' Emily

Penne returned her attention to her guest. 'You must be very tired dear as it's middle of the night by American time. We're five hours or so ahead here I believe.'

'Yes. I shall have to adjust to the time difference for a day or so. But I don't feel a bit tired. I did sleep a little on the flight.' The warm personality of Emily Penne made Sally Lane feel even more badly about deceiving her. She had taken an instant dislike to Martha Oakes and as she followed the silent black clad figure up the wide staircase a small shiver touched her spine. She felt something more than the chill of the country air.

After depositing the luggage in the room that had been chosen for the guest Charlie put away the Bentley. Then he strolled about the garden for a while to allow the two enough time to greet each other. Emily Penne had especially asked him to join them when the girl arrived. He made his way now into the drawing room.

'I think she'll like the room we've put her in Charlie. It overlooks a particularly nice aspect of the garden. What a pity she didn't come in summer when the flowers are out. Still I must be grateful that she's here at all at long last. Thank you for collecting her. I dare say she's feeling disorientated time-wise. We shall have a dinner party on Saturday to give her a special welcome to Grandstone House. Clive will be home this weekend so we'll be seven in number with Alice, John and Lydie. I've tried to persuade Martha to join us but for some reason she never will nowadays. She used to when William was alive, although not when we had guests. She says that she can't serve and eat. I've often suggested that we could hire help when we have dinner parties but she won't hear of it. She likes to be in charge of the kitchen.'

Just as well the sour-faced old cat didn't want to join them at the table, her sombre presence always put a damper on things Charlie thought. 'We'll take your niece for a drive on Saturday morning.'

'I shall look forward to it Charlie. Clive is collecting Lydie but apparently they are going straight to Tanglewood. They're not stopping here on the way because they want to give Paula time to get her breath back and adjust after the journey. They'll be arriving half an hour before dinner time. Clive telephoned me this morning.'

Before Charlie could respond to this Sally Lane returned.

She had changed into a woollen dress of soft rose-pink colour. Her small dainty figure was in bright contrast to the large boned one of dark-clad Martha Oakes who had followed her into the room with a tea-tray.

★ ★ ★

'We'll take Paula on a tour of the estate later Charlie,' Emily Penne said after breakfast as he was leaving the room.

'A pleasure,' he replied smiling.

In the garden he puffed at his pipe thoughtfully as he performed his various tasks. With this belated visit of the niece bang went his own hopes. Up until now he hadn't imagined that anyone used to a place such as New York would want to settle permanently in the quiet English countryside. Now having met the girl he wasn't so sure. She was of a much quieter disposition than he had expected her to be.

Ever since the arrival of a registered letter, which Emily Penne had opened herself after selecting it from the rest of the mail, he had been curious as to the contents. Since it bore the stamp of a solicitor he assumed that it had some bearing on her will. Perhaps an alteration. He had a distinct feeling that there would be a condition concerning the inheritance of the house and estate which would require the beneficiary to live on the property. Emily Penne had made it clear that she did not want the house sold after her death. Although he had lived at Grandstone House for barely seven months himself so far he had come to love the old place and its gardens and already felt a possessiveness. He paused to straighten up as an idea came to him. He exhaled St. Bruno smoke and smiled round the stem of the pipe. With a bit of luck on his side he might be able to persuade the girl into marriage with him. There might still be hopes of his becoming a real country squire — if she was willing.

★　★　★

In the village Martha Oakes parked her old upright against the kerb outside the cottage of her widowed sister. 'Are you home Mary?' she called as she entered. The unlocked door was no indication since this was always left so when her sister slipped out to the shops. As she walked through to the kitchen at the back she showed surprise at seeing the shampoo lathered head bent over a large enamelled bowl on the table. 'Funny time to be washing your hair, Saturday morning!'

'Oh hello Marth. Sara Jenkins asked me if I'd like to attend the Christening of her Laura's baby. They're having a bit of a do afterwards. Only asked me yesterday evening.

If I'd had more warning I would have washed my hair yesterday morning. No good doing it in the evenings it takes too long to dry — you know how thick it is. I must get myself a hair drier. Will you pour the rinsing water over for me?'

Martha Oakes picked up the large enamel jug of warm water placed ready and as she slowly poured it evenly over the bent head she spoke. 'She's arrived — the niece.'

'Has she now! I expect you barely recognise her. She was only a child when she last visited wasn't she?'

'Hummp, and a precocious little madam at that. She made a fuss because I didn't place her cutlery left handed. She seems to have quietened down a bit from what I've noticed so far. She's only here now to make sure she doesn't get her nose put out of joint where the will's concerned. The moment they wrote her a letter saying that *she* was ill a reply came to say she was coming for a visit. Getting worried about *him* worming his way in favour I shouldn't wonder. She even got *him* to write the letter. *She* probably told the niece how he fusses over her. Fawns more like. Obviously only took the job for what he thinks he can get out of it. Properly taken her in. She's nothing but a silly old fool who revels in the attention.'

Mary squeezed the excess water from her hair then reached for the towel beside the bowl and straightened up. Her sister's spoken emphasis on *her* and *him* enabled her to identify the person referred to. From experience she was aware that Martha never indicated people by name if she disliked them. Mary knew that this included the young man who had taken up residence in Grandstone House. And long ago she had known that her sister had no affection for Emily Penneston-Barkley. Mary had detected an element of envy in this. Perhaps even jealousy; and she'd always had a good idea as to why. Years ago she had suspected that Martha was sweet on Emily's husband William. Even as a child Mary had never understood her sister's unsociable ways. Even back then she had been laconic, withdrawn and solitary, just as she was now.

'*He* knew what he was about when he took on the job. If you can call it that. Behaves as if he owns the place.'

'But he couldn't have known how wealthy she is when he applied for the position Marth.' Mary was now rubbing her head vigorously with the towel. She knew that her sister expected to be favoured in Emily Penne's will herself, and recognised the resentment that a newcomer might do so.

'Huh not much! *She* wouldn't care if he is a crook so long as she's fussed over like she always was by William. Always has been spoiled. *He* gives her the attention she wants. Anyone can see it's him in that newspaper photo. *She* doesn't *want* to see it. Told me off for going to George Hill about it. I've a good mind to show it to the niece.'

'I should leave well alone if I were you Marth.' Mary wrapped the towel about her head as she spoke. 'You've had a good position there all these years, don't risk it by creating mischief.' She picked up the bowl of sudsy water and went through to the garden to empty it over the plants, relieving herself briefly from the glum countenance of her sister and the disagreeable remarks. Although Mary had always been an available ear to the many grouses of the past, the cheerless company of Martha always cast a temporary gloom upon her own spirits.

Now, as always, she felt sorry for her strange and taciturn sister on whose life the sun apparently never seemed to shine.

12

With concealed interest Charlie watched the
girl he knew as Paula Carpenter re-arrange
the silver cutlery beside her plate. Each
mealtime since her arrival he had noticed her
perform this same change over to the
right-hand side before eating. At first he had
wondered why Martha Oakes came to
repeatedly set the place at the dining table
incorrectly. They each kept to the same
position at the table every day. Something
nudged at his memory as he proceeded to
eat.

'Now don't linger over dinner on my
account this evening,' Emily Penne was
saying. 'When you've both finished you must
go or you'll be late for the theatre.'

'Yes — yes of course,' Charlie responded,
his mind still on the knife and fork in the
dainty hands opposite him. 'Good of you to
have the dinner served early for our benefit.'
While he was speaking something clicked in
his memory; the letter that he'd read from the
bundle in the bureau that day when Emily
Penne had fallen asleep in the garden. He
probed his recollection deeper. What were the

words exactly? Something about . . . tennis . . . a sprained wrist. A good thing that she was left-handed so able to write the letter. Left handed! Fascinated now he stared at her hands until she glanced up. He returned his attention to his plate. There was probably no mystery about it. No doubt she was ambidextrous. Yet, on further reflection he thought it strange that Martha Oakes should continually set the place for a left handed eater; which meant that she too remembered.

13

NEW YORK

'Hell I needed that.' James Maddison muttered after tossing down whisky from a glass in one swig. With all the questions, the courtrooms, and two funerals behind him he needed that, and some. He poured another measure and carried this across the lounge-room of the apartment that he had shared with his late wife. At present it was still in her name and on the market for sale. The proceeds, according to her will, were to go to charity along with all her other financial interests. 'Bitch!' he spat out the word, as he'd done so often since this unexpected discovery.

His hand now resting on the telephone he stood in deep contemplation as he prepared himself for his next move. Paula Carpenter had been buried as Sally Lane. It had been an open and shut case even though he'd had a sticky time with his story to the police. But he was now satisfied that he had handled it all well. Sally Lane, he had told them, had arrived at the apartment where she had arranged to stay while Paula was overseas. In ignorance of this fact, Cora had shot Sally in error; a clear case of mistaken identity. It had been necessary to admit that Paula was his mistress at the time of the shooting. There had been a few nasty moments when it looked as if the police were going to contact England to 'break the news to Miss Carpenter.' But he'd managed to convince them that he must be the one to do this on account that the girls had been such close friends with each other, and the shock etc . . .

This breaking of the news he had delayed until now. He had decided it best to let this wait until Sally Lane was settled in at the country house. Then there would be less chance that she would panic and run; worse still that she would return to New York. Established in the household as Paula she would have no choice but to continue with the deception. Before she had left New York they had agreed that she must not write for a few weeks, and to take care that nobody saw the address on the envelope when she eventually did so. If she needed any information meanwhile she was to telephone Paula's apartment and reverse the charges. 'And,' he had instructed her, 'make damn sure you're not overheard.' So far no letter had arrived. However he didn't know whether she had tried to phone the apartment at all. He had spent very little time there himself since the murder. He knew that she hadn't phoned the offices. He'd had serious worries about that in case she did so and gave her name to the switchboard operator or the receptionist, since all these people were mourning her death.

When the police had finished in the apartment that had been Paula's he had given up the lease and removed all the belongings. He had stored them at a new apartment on which he'd taken a temporary lease while he sorted things out. This task was now complete. The furniture, the clothes and effects that had belonged to the two girls he had disposed of along with all the other items left by Sally Lane. From now on she would have to remain in England as Paula Carpenter. Sally Lane was dead and buried and could never be resurrected. He put down his empty glass, picked up the receiver, and dialled.

★　★　★

The telephone rang when Sally Lane was halfway up the stairs on her way to fetch a woollen jacket for the weather had turned cold. The extension in the upstairs corridor was closest to hand. She had just left Emily Penne in the drawing room and Charlie had gone into the village to get the gardening shears sharpened.

Martha Oakes was dusting and polishing in the library. This room was not the domestic territory of the maid who came in two days a week. She had just picked up a small basket that contained dusters and polish having completed her work and was about to leave the room. As she reached the door the phone rang and she turned back to answer. She picked up the receiver at the same time as Sally Lane and before she could speak she heard the American voice on the line.

'Hello — Paula Carp . . . '

'James here,' he cut in, 'are you alone?'

'Why hello James! I thought we . . . '

His voice cut her short. 'Can you be overheard?'

'Just a moment,' she put down the receiver and went to the head of the stairs to look down into the deserted hall where she could see the telephone in its cradle.

She returned to the phone. 'It's all right to talk James. Everything is fine. Tell Paula and . . . '

His voice interrupted rudely. 'Stop talking and listen carefully and prepare yourself for a shock. Something terrible has happened here.

162

Before I tell you remember that it's important for you to stay calm. Now are you ready — Paula is dead. Cora shot her the day you left.'

Sally Lane gasped loudly and groped for the nearby chair. Slowly she sat down, her eyes staring at the phone as if it contained some evil spirit. 'No! No — !' she protested against the words.

'Now take hold of yourself,' his voice commanded sharply. 'And for the sake of your own bloody neck listen good.'

Down in the library Martha Oakes was listening good herself.

When James Maddison had related the rest of the dreadful facts he paused briefly. Sally Lane glanced wildly about her as if for some means of escape before the demon voice could speak again and confirm that she was not dreaming some hideous nightmare.

'You okay? Are you listening?' His tone was impatient now. When there was no immediate response he continued irritably. 'For Christ sake say something. I don't know whether you're there or not!'

She made an attempt to speak but only a choked sound emerged.

'Okay — okay. I guess the shock has been too much. But don't the hell do anything crazy. You understand that I must see you

163

urgently to discuss what's to be done next. Remember it's important that you stay put and say nothing of this to anyone. We'll both be in deep trouble if you do. I'm coming over to England at the end of next week. I shall telephone you to arrange a meeting when I arrive. There is a lot involved and some matters I still have to clear up here.'

With a concentrated effort Sally Lane forced her voice.

'Paula left her car for repair somewhere.'

'That was no problem. The garage telephoned the office to say it was ready to collect. I've done that. It didn't affect the police enquiries; they think they've been dealing with the murder of Sally Lane who doesn't own one.'

In the library Martha Oakes replaced the receiver unconcerned now about any telltale click. That dominant American male voice had compelled her to listen in. Although the conversation had been almost totally one-sided she had heard much more than expected. A bombshell had landed in her lap so to speak and when she was over the shock herself she would decide what to do with it. Stunned she sat down on the leather couch to digest what she'd overheard. Unused to such stimulating elements in her life she felt intoxicated and lifted out of her usual misanthropic state. To learn that the American visitor in the house was an impostor posing as the niece was shock enough; but the trick had turned into serious law breaking! Gradually the information incited her to act. Her mind was already calculating on how she could turn it to her own advantage and at the same time do Charlie so-called Baines in the eye.

Still too overwrought and in shock for the moment to return to the drawing room Sally Lane stood at her bedroom window looking down over the garden. She made a concentrated effort to calm herself enough to arrange some clear thoughts from the present chaos in her mind. Mad! James Maddison must have been mad to go to such lengths to cover up what, by comparison, had been only a light hearted deception to please an old lady. No harm had been intended. No gain to herself other than pure enjoyment of being here in the English countryside fulfilling a dream by simply standing in for Paula. It had been an answer to Paula continually disappointing the lone relative to whom the visit meant so much.

Although the serious offence of travelling on a false passport had been committed it would have been by far the best thing to have owned up and taken the consequences.

Particularly in as much as James Maddison himself was concerned. So why had he made these complications? She knew his character. She had observed his ruthless tactics in business affairs, and wondered at his motives now. Some decision was necessary. Paula was no longer here to back up her story if she confessed. The guilt was hers alone to bear. What if she went quietly away? To the continent perhaps where nobody knew her. Tell Emily that she had no wish to inherit. But that would not sound feasible and would invite questions which she was unable to answer, and explanations she could not give. To admit the truth was not possible. The shock of Paula's murder could prove too traumatic, even fatal to Emily in her fragile state of health. Perhaps it was best to keep silent about it all and let things take their course.

When the inheritance eventually passed to her she could give it to charity, a children's home or hospital. That would absolve her conscience by turning wrong to something worthwhile. Grandstone House she could make over to Charlie.

James Maddison had committed the worst, and unforgivable, deception without her knowledge or consent and forced her into further mendacity. In her absence he had involved her inextricably in a deliberately criminal act. Why had he gone to such lengths? Fear of him now gripped her as the answer to this question dawned. The inheritance! Money was of prime concern to him. His life seemed excessively bound to finance and the business of Maddison Enterprises. Because of his greed she was involved through no fault of her own. There was no reversal of what he had done without incriminating herself. Nobody would believe that she had not been party to the mad act that he'd carried out by falsely identifying Paula's body.

From now on she would be under his continual pressure. She shuddered at the thought of seeing him again and wished that he were not coming.

She rested her burning forehead against the cold window pane and saw Charlie returning in the Bentley. Moments later as he came towards the house he glanced up as if sensing her there. He waved. With automatic response she listlessly lifted her hand. Briefly she was seized by an impulse to rush down to him and confess everything and ask his advice. He looked so dependable. Desperately she craved his support and comfort right now. She resisted the moment. What could he do? He would never forgive her if he thought that she'd done anything to hurt Emily. His concern for the old lady was genuine despite what Paula had said about his motives being suspect. If anyone deserved to benefit from the inheritance it was certainly Charlie. She watched him until he was out of her view. To leave would mean never to see him again. At present she badly needed a friend, even if she could not confide in him. She could see no other course for her future other than to go on living under the protective roof of Grandstone House; living a lie until the death of Emily Penne after which she could put things right. At present she would give much to be able to share her grief over Paula's death with someone. James Maddison it seemed felt none.

She realised now that she had always known he had a ruthless streak in his character. Often she had wondered secretly what Paula found attractive about him. Perhaps it was just that Paula had needed a dominant masterful man simply because of her own strong personality. She would have considered a man less so to be weak. Yet because of his philandering ways she had met an early and violent death. Paula, so young and vital, dead at twenty three. It was shocking and hard to believe.

The sound of a door opening and closing

broke into her thoughts as Charlie entered his bedroom. Again she had an impulse, almost overwhelming, to run to him with her fears. She heard his door open again and close and heard the muffled sound of his feet on the carpet as he went towards the stairs. She came from her room and could not quite control the tremor in her voice as she called, 'Charlie.'

He paused and turned to glance back. Her impulse faded. How could she tell him? He looked so honest.

Smiling he waited expectantly. But she merely said, 'I guess it must be almost lunchtime.' She joined him and they went downstairs together.

That evening at dinner Emily Penne announced that she did not feel well and was not hungry.

'Perhaps you should lie down for a while.' Charlie stood up from the table ready to assist her. 'I'll help you to your room.'

'Not yet Charlie thank you. I don't wish to disrupt dinner. I shall be fine until you've both finished.' She saw his anxious look and gave a wan smile. 'I'll be all right — really.'

Sally Lane also was not hungry and barely touched her meal. Emily Penne noticed this and asked, 'Are you feeling unwell dear?'

'I'm fine — really. A cold perhaps coming

on.' Sally Lane tried to erase the visible signs of shock and forced herself to voice a few trivial remarks.

When Charlie had finished dinner he assisted Emily up to her room. Sally Lane followed and remained to help her prepare for bed.

'Come back in fifteen minutes Charlie and you can both sit and talk to me for a while,' Emily Penne said.

At the door Charlie turned back to say, 'I think I should call Doctor Macalistair.'

'Not tonight Charlie. Wait and see how I feel tomorrow. I'm just a little tired that's all.'

'The wind was too keen yesterday. You would insist on going outside.'

'I know. But it was worth it. The viburnum is so lovely at this time of the year.'

Sally Lane helped her prepare for bed. Ten minutes later as she eased herself back against the propped up pillows she said, 'I suppose you've fallen in love with him already?'

Despite her plaguing anxieties Sally Lane smiled and replied, 'You're trying to match-make.'

A distinct wistfulness sounded in the old lady's tone as she replied, 'I hope so dear. I do hope so.'

An hour later when she was asleep they left her room. As they were about to go downstairs the telephone rang. The sudden shrill sound startled Sally Lane and she darted to the closest extension in the upstairs corridor. Her trembling hands snatched up the receiver. 'Hello,' her voice sounded hoarse to her ears.

Charlie waited expecting the call to be from Lydie. He could see by the expression on Sally Lane's face that it was not and continued on downstairs. On reaching the hall he heard a door closing and his eyes were drawn to the telephone cord still swinging slightly from recent disturbance. For a few seconds he stood staring at it before shrugging and moving on. No doubt Martha Oakes had attempted to answer the call.

★　★　★

Doctor Macalistair seated himself in a chair beside the bed to write a prescription. He tore the page from the pad and placed it on the bedside table. 'It's advisable for you to stay in bed for a day or two Emily. I'll call in a couple of days.' He held out the prescription slip to Sally Lane seated on the chaise. 'Ask Charlie to collect this from the chemist and see that your aunt takes it every four hours. It'll ease the congestion.'

Sally Lane took the slip. 'I will Doctor.'

Charlie was waiting for him down in the hall. 'How is she Doctor? Is it her chest again?'

'Fraid so Charlie. I've given her orders to stay abed for a couple of days. I suppose she still likes to take her walks around the garden despite the weather?'

Charlie nodded. 'Several times a day now if it isn't actually raining.'

'Well try to dissuade her during the worst of winter. I don't suppose she'll mind so much being confined to the house now that she has her niece here for company. Pretty girl. Quiet too. Changed a lot since I last saw her. She didn't remember me at all, which is a little surprising. When she was here last I had to treat her for measles and I recall her telling me that I looked exactly like her headmaster at school.'

'Too long ago no doubt,' Charlie replied as he saw the doctor out.

14

From her bedroom window Sally Lane saw James Maddison arrive in a hired car. Since his last telephone call she had waited, still in shock and nervously impatient, for his arrival. There were so many questions to be answered concerning the death of Paula. Not liking the idea of his coming to the house, she would have preferred the meeting to have been elsewhere. But he had given no choice. She wished that she'd been more assertive about this now as she hurried downstairs. She was outside before he reached the front door. Her acute dislike of him prevented her from making some preliminary greeting. She came straight to the point. 'We can talk in the summer house. I haven't told anyone that you were coming. Charlie has gone into town thank heaven and Mrs Penne is sleeping. The housekeeper is about but I'm not sure where at this moment. Follow me.' Still out of breath from her rush down the stairs and partly from anger she led the way round the side of the house and across the frosty lawn.

They caught the attention of Martha Oakes as they passed within view of the sewing room where she was at present ironing. She showed no surprise for she'd listened in on two of the telephone calls since that first one. One she had missed out on because Charlie had been close at hand to the phone that time. She was aware that a meeting was to be arranged but had expected this to take place away from the house. She deduced that it had been discussed during the call which she'd missed. She had heard a car arrive but thought it to be the Bentley returning.

For several seconds she watched the two crossing the garden and guessed which spot they were heading for. She grabbed two tea-cloths from the laundry pile and dashed into the kitchen to soak them under the tap, then snatched up some pegs.

The washing line, situated obscurely for aesthetic reasons rather than convenience, was at the rear of the summer house behind screening shrubs.

Caught by the icy breeze her wet hands froze and stung as she made her way inconspicuously along the paved path rather than take the quicker route across the lawn and risk being seen. Hidden now behind a large bush she was within earshot of the loud-toned American voices.

Sally Lane was speaking, her voice high with recrimination. 'But why did you tell the

174

police it was me that Cora had shot? Why? Why lie about something so serious! The truth would have made no difference to you, or affected you at all!'

'If I'd admitted it was Paula you'd have been in trouble for impersonating her and travelling on her passport.'

'I could have explained how that came about. I should have admitted that Paula asked me to make this visit in her place because she didn't want to come herself and didn't want to disappoint her aunt.'

'Do you really expect anyone would believe such a tale?' James Maddison scoffed.

'It's not a tale it's the truth! It's quite obvious that Paula agreed. How else would I know about her aunt and this place and be in possession of her passport and birth certificate?'

With deliberate intent to create doubts he remained silent leaving the question suspended on her frost misted breath. More distressed now she continued. 'For God's sake why did you complicate things like this! There seems no reason. You certainly didn't do it for me. Travelling on another persons' passport is not such a crime as falsely identifying a dead person, especially one who has been murdered. Poor Paula! You should've telephoned me as soon as I arrived

175

here. Instead you deliberately kept me in ignorance. I want to know the reason why . . . '

He cut in showing irritation at what he obviously thought of as her naivety, 'Isn't it obvious to you yet! We couldn't pass up an opportunity like this. Now that Paula is not here the inheritance will probably go to the Baines guy if you don't claim it. Have you any idea how much the old lady is worth?'

She glared at him, her repugnance showing. 'I do not know, nor do I wish to. It's no business of mine. So far I've caused no real harm. In fact I've saved Paula's aunt from the shocking news of her death. What do you think that could do to her considering her age and state of health.' She paused to suppress a sob before continuing. 'How can you think of gain when such a dreadful thing has happened. It just goes to show how little you really thought of Paula.'

Unperturbed he rose from the seat. Swinging his arms across his chest for warmth he went to stand at the entrance of the summer house, from which point he cast a speculative gaze over the house. 'I figure the old place must be worth a small fortune.'

Her dislike turned to loathing. The very last thing she wanted was that he should profit from his despicable actions. From her desperation an idea occurred which, although an outright lie, would at least kill off his mercenary designs on Grandstone House. 'Paula's aunt has already willed the house to Charlie.'

'What!' He swung round to face her. 'That Baines jerk! The gardener? Did she tell you that?'

She took a deep breath prepared to lie further. 'Yes the other day when he was out.'

'F . . . Does he know that?'

She winced at his bad language and replied stiffly, 'No.'

'And what did you say to that? You're supposed to be her niece for God's sake! Paula would have had plenty to say. The guy's almost a stranger. You can't let her do it. You must protest. Talk to her. Make her change her mind. Tell her *you* want the house. Do it right away or she might get too ill to do anything about it. At her age and in her condition she could snuff it anytime.'

'How can you be so heartless!' She looked at him in disgust. 'I'll do no such thing. Charlie deserves the house and he's more entitled than I. At least he isn't a fraud!'

'The hell he isn't,' he snorted. 'Why do you imagine he took on the work here. You're as naive as the old lady.'

'You have made it impossible for me to

confess the truth of how and why I came to be here, but when the time comes I can and will do some good with the inheritance that would have been Paula's. I intend to arrange for the money to go to a children's charity. I shall not benefit in any way. And the house *will* be Charlie's'

'Are you out of your mind! He has less right to it than you. Have you overlooked the fact that you are at least related to Paula and on her death all her property should pass to you by law.'

'I haven't forgotten that Paula was my half-sister but I would never wish to gain from her death.'

His anger rose at this opposition to his plans. He was used to grappling orally and mentally with the best business-heads around and getting his way. 'And what about the housekeeper? What has she to say about it? She's been here for years from what I understand. She's not going to be any too pleased when she finds out that he's been favoured above her considering he's been here only a few months.'

'The house would not have gone to Martha in any case. Paula's aunt told me that she has provided for her to buy a small cottage. Apparently she has no dependents and would not want a large house just for herself.' This piece of information Sally Lane could relate with truth since Emily Penne had told her as much one afternoon in the garden. It had been meant for her ears only. But in the circumstances it was not likely to go any further.

'You still haven't told me yet how wealthy she is. Has she mentioned the extent of the inheritance apart from the house which you can still arrange back in your favour.'

'I have no idea and I certainly will do no such thing as even mention the house to her.' Something that he'd said earlier struck her. At the time, still distressed, she had let it pass without comment. 'You said just now that *we* couldn't pass up an opportunity like this. What did you mean by *we*. Why are you so interested in the inheritance?'

He moved away from the entrance and went to stand before her, his hand resting on her shoulder.

Angrily she shook it off and rose from the seat, her eyes challenging. 'What exactly did you mean?'

'Calm down honey. I meant precisely what I said. We can't toss away an opportunity like this. You'll get what would have gone to Paula and we'll split down the middle. And that includes this house. You have only to tell her that you want to live here.'

'I'll do no such thing!' she flung back at him. 'Understand this — I shall claim nothing because I want nothing by cheating. Now get out of here.' She made a move towards the entrance but was stopped by his quiet but menacing tone.

'You will honey. I haven't gone to all this trouble for . . . '

She swung round and cut his words short. 'It's no use threatening me. I've already made it clear that I'd rather tell the truth.'

'The truth?' his tone had turned mocking now. 'And what is the truth for Jesus sake! I mean — if you tell them your story I should be obliged to tell them mine. About how we plotted together to have Paula murdered by egging Cora on knowing she was unstable enough to do it.'

'That's an absurd idea and you know it. If you think you can bluff me into believing that you'd put your neck on the line just to spite me, with nothing to gain in the end, then you really are mad, and I *do* mean insane!'

Resentment at this inference by a mere typist in his employ showed in his steel-cold eyes. His fist itched to strike out at her. He calmed the impulse and studied her determined expression. Then decided to try another tack — a different angle. 'Okay — okay. So for some goddamn reason you want to tell the old girl that her niece was murdered, that for the past five weeks you've been hoodwinking her and that Paula was party to the trick in order to cop the estate. Okay — okay I'm all for it. In fact I'll do the talking. No time like the present. I'll do it right now. The Baines guy'll laugh all the way to the cemetery when the old girl snuffs it in shock.'

She leaned against the pillared support of the arched entrance. Her heart was beating fast with anger. 'My God! To think that Paula died because of you.' Her tone held contempt and horror.

At this point Martha Oakes retreated from the cover of the shrubs and edged back to the washing line where she hung the two soaked tea-cloths. An air of controlled excitement moved with her stiff figure across the frost-crisped lawn, heedless now of the biting wind and her stinging finger tips. As she closed the door of the sewing room behind her she glanced back at the two figures, slightly bowed against the elements, hurrying away from the summer house. The startling fruits of her eavesdropping had placed a whip in her hand and already her mind was speculating on how she could use it.

Just lately the old fool upstairs was a magnet for impostors. So she was leaving the house to Charlie Barnes was she! She resumed the ironing. 'Well we'll soon see about changing that,' she muttered, thumping the iron down and across a pillow case.

When Charlie arrived back from the bank in town James Maddison had left. After garaging the Bentley he went straight into the library to put the cheque book and accompanying papers into a drawer of the desk. Without first removing his top-coat he sat down on the leather couch to think. This was the second time in the past two months that the old lady had been unwell. If anything happened to her he'd be out on his ear. Again he wondered whether that letter addressed to her solicitor which she had asked him to send off by registered post had been in some way connected with changes to her will.

If in the past her niece had given the impression that she would never come to live permanently in the house when the time came to inherit, she must surely have changed her mind. It was quite clear now that she really liked the old place.

It would come hard to leave and start again in some strange place. He couldn't hope to strike so lucky again. There could never be anywhere quite like Grandstone House and estate. Just lately he had been mulling over a decision to tell Emily the truth about his own life. To confess that he had deliberately set out to give a wrong impression about himself.

At the beginning he hadn't anticipated that he would grow fond of the old girl and have a conscience about deceiving her. He felt confident that the attachment which she felt for him would withstand her disappointment. After all — she had refused to pay any heed to Martha Oakes and the newspaper cutting back in the summer. Only recently she had said that his being there was, for her, a sort of compensation for the son she and her William had never had.

She appreciated the time and attention that he unstintingly gave outside the sphere of the duties for which she had originally employed him. True, at first, he had set out to contrive such a bond. Now he wanted to be sure that her approval of him would withstand knowing the real Charlie.

Desperately he wanted to own Grandstone House one day. By now she knew how genuinely attached he had become to the old place. Not for its monetary value, but for its intrinsic beauty and for the gardens where he had so diligently toiled. He felt the need to let her know that he was not the well-to-do down-on-his-luck chap that he had led her to believe, but a penniless product from the back-streets of Dockland who just happened to have the right sort of looks and acquired social finesse.

His mind made up he rose from the couch and stopping only to remove his top-coat and hang it on the hall-stand made his way up to her room.

The door was almost wide open. He knocked lightly. Her bed faced the door and from where she lay she could see him. 'Come in Charlie I *am* awake. I think I must have nodded off which means I probably won't sleep tonight. Come and sit down. Is it very cold outside today?'

'It is rather. Frost still on the ground.' He seated himself on a chair beside the bed.

'I don't think I've ever seen you looking so serious Charlie. Is something worrying you? I certainly hope you're not concerned about me. Actually I feel a lot better today.'

He was silent for a few moments while he tried to find the right words to begin. To make a simple statement would be the best he decided. 'Emily there's something I want to tell you — about myself. I'm not . . . '

Before he could get any further she shook her head and smiled. 'No Charlie. There's nothing I need to know about you — really.'

'But I must. You don't understand . . . you see I'm not . . . '

At this point she reached up and removed

her hearing-aid and placed it on the bed-covers. 'I'm not listening Charlie,' she told him firmly. Then chuckled at the expression on is face.

He smiled despite the unexpected thwarting of his confession. Then he sighed and squeezed the hand resting on the counterpane closest to him.

The voice of the doctor floated up from the hall. Charlie stood up instantly and pointed in the direction of the door as he mouthed, 'Doctor Macalistair.' Not knowing whether she understood without her hearing-aid which was still on the bed.

He went to the top of the stairs and greeted the doctor who was already on his way up. 'Hello Doctor. Emily is awake.'

'Good-day Charlie. How is she?'

'Perked up a bit today. Although she didn't have a particularly restful night apparently.'

The doctor entered the bedroom. Frowning now Charlie continued on his way downstairs to wait in the hall. Why had she stopped him from speaking about himself he wondered?

Five minutes later he was still pondering on this as the doctor handed him a prescription slip. 'Just a few mild sleeping pills for while she's abed. Should have her up before

Christmas though.'

'Good. I'll go and pick these up from the chemist.' Charlie collected his top-coat from the stand.

Martha suddenly appeared and saw the doctor out. He held up the hearing aid. 'A little accident I'm afraid Martha. I trod on it. Didn't see it underfoot. It must have fallen off the bed. I'm taking it in for repair. Might take a day or so. All depends. She'll feel a little isolated without it. She needs a spare really. I'll telephone later to let you know how long it's going to take. See that she stays in bed and keeps warm. Nippy weather today.' He drew his coat collar up as he stepped out the front door.

A moment later Charlie re-entered the bedroom and held up the prescription slip, making a sign that he was going out to the village to collect it.

Emily Penne smiled and nodded. Charlie went downstairs.

As he went towards the front door Sally Lane came in. 'Enjoy your walk?' he asked.

'Yes thank you Charlie. It's awful cold though. I saw the doctor leaving. I'm sorry I wasn't back in time. I had meant to be. Has her chest improved?'

'A little, according to the doctor. I think she looks a lot brighter.'

'She was asleep when I left the house or I shouldn't have gone.'

'Yes I know that. But you need to get out for exercise sometimes. She's been dozing a lot during the daytime just lately. I'm just off to collect this.' Charlie held up the slip of paper. 'Mild sleeping pills while she's confined to bed. Shouldn't be for too long though.' He moved on out the door. Sally Lane closed it behind him.

Too upset to stay in the house after James Maddison had left she had felt a need to walk and had gone for a long stroll to be alone to think.

Right now she was in desperate need of moral support and even advice. The ghastly secret was too much to bear alone. During her walk she had again toyed with the idea of telling Charlie, unburdening herself. But had decided that it would not be fair, and would be to no good purpose to involve him in the deceit.

She felt real fear now. James Maddison would be back and she was sure that he was hatching some evil plot. No amount of thinking had come up with a way of freeing herself from his threats other than by a full confession to Emily Penne. And he had already pointed out the possible consequences of doing that.

After removing her coat and hanging it in her wardrobe she went along to Emily Penne's room. With a forced smile of greeting ready on her lips she entered. When she saw that the old lady's eyes were closed and she was dozing she tiptoed out.

She went downstairs to the drawing room where she seated herself in the window staring out at the garden.

* * *

As Charlie drove into the village he saw Doctor Macalistair's car parked outside one of the cottages. He drew up alongside and wound down his window just as the doctor emerged from the front door. 'I say Doctor,' he called, 'can I drop the hearing aid off to save you a journey.'

'I'd be much obliged Charlie.' The doctor removed one glove and produced the device from a pocket in his top-coat. 'Lindsays in the High Street. Nobody in the village does this sort of repair work unfortunately.' He handed the hearing aid through the open window.

'I gathered that Doctor. Perhaps they can fix it while I wait.'

'Thanks Charlie. Give me a call if it has to be collected later, and I'll pick it up.'

188

'Will do.' Charlie closed his window and drove on.

Less than an hour later he was back at Grandstone House with the hearing-aid in his pocket. The instrument had not been badly damaged and the necessary repair work had been done while Charlie waited.

When he handed it to Emily Penne she looked delighted. 'Oh that's marvellous Charlie. I did feel so cut off without it and it's so tiresome for everyone else.' She placed the aid in her ear. 'Now sit down and tell me the latest plans for Christmas and how long Lydie will be able to stay. Is she free to come this weekend as well after all?'

'Yes she can. She's been working extra nights so that she can be free. I've arranged to collect her on Saturday morning because Clive can't get away this weekend.' Charlie seated himself on a chair close to the bed. 'Lydie has two whole weeks holiday starting on the 23rd.'

'And are you sure she can spend the whole time here with us?'

'Quite certain.' Even as he spoke her eyelids drooped and she dozed contentedly.

Quietly Charlie left the room and went downstairs to check the garden for any frost damaged plants.

This was just the moment for which

Martha Oakes had been waiting. When she saw Charlie pass the kitchen window on his way to the vegetable garden she removed her apron. She had serious business in mind and an apron seemed a psychological disadvantage for presenting her terms of silence.

When she went into the hall she saw Sally Lane going up the stairs. She followed and was close on her heels when she entered Emily Penne's room.

'I think we have something to discuss Miss *Sally Lane*.' She put strong emphasis on the name.

With a loud gasp Sally Lane swung round startled; as much by the unexpected voice so close as by the confrontation itself.

'Caught you off-guard did I Miss Lane?'

There was a slight movement from the bed and Sally Lane turned briefly in its direction.

'No need to bother about *her*. The doctor trod on her hearing aid and it's out for repair.' Martha Oakes added spitefully, 'She's as deaf as a post without it.'

Emily Penne's head was at an angle on the pillow and her face turned away from their direction. The aid in her ear was not visible.

'So,' continued Martha Oakes, 'her niece was murdered was she!'

Sally Lane was white-faced with shock. 'How did you find that out!'

Martha Oakes, who did not intend to waste time answering the obvious, ignored the question and continued. 'Why the sneaky meeting outside in the summer house? Why didn't you bring your American accomplice into the house? The three of us could have had an interesting discussion in the library to our mutual benefit.'

'Obviously you've not only been eavesdropping on my phone calls but spying on me as well. You are despicable! I'll repeat what you have probably already heard me say. I shall do nothing that would harm Emily in any way. I did not come here for personal gain. Paula begged me to visit in her place because she didn't want to come herself. I was badly shocked by her death. She was my half sister and we were very much alike in looks.'

'So I gather. But — as your friend said — who would believe such a story.'

'How dare you! It's the truth. Paula was shot and killed by his wife after I had left New York to come here. He did not tell me the dreadful news until almost five weeks later. I loved Paula. She was afraid that her aunt might leave the house to Charlie because her letter indicated that she was becoming attached to him. Since I've been here I've grown very fond of Emily. She's a lovely person and I would not risk telling her

191

the news about Paula. The shock would be too great for her now. When the time comes I shall transfer all I receive in Paula's name over to Charlie. And I mean *everything*. Is that clear Miss Oakes?'

'If you think I'll keep quiet and let that parasite benefit you can think again Miss Sally Lane.'

'How dare you speak about him like that! Charlie has a genuine affection for Emily despite the short time he's known her. You evidently have none even after all the years you've been employed here.'

'Taken a fancy to his pretty face have you? I should have thought one phoney would recognise another.'

'You are the phoney Miss Oakes. You have lived here all those years concealing your true feelings towards the person who has given you a home in this lovely house. Why did you stay so long if you dislike Emily so much.'

'I should have thought that obvious. How else could I live like this. I could never have hoped to own such a place myself. As for *her* — she's always had too much of everything. Spoiled all her life. Too much attention, especially from her William. Dinner parties — fine clothes. Never had to do a day's work in her life. Well I couldn't care less about her.

And I assure you that I'd spring this on her without hesitation.'

'You must have always been envious of her.'

Martha Oakes shrugged. 'I don't care what you think Miss.'

'You seem to have found your tongue all of a sudden. Why now? And — since you dislike Emily so much what prevented you from telling her what you overheard by eavesdropping on her guest's private phone calls?'

'I have other ideas. I want to speak with your American friend. Bring him here to the house for a discussion that will be to our mutual benefit.'

'I shall do no such thing. I'll not be party to blackmail. You can't frighten me.' Sally Lane attempted to stifle the tremor in her voice despite the brave words.

Martha Oakes ignored this and a slight movement from the bed went unnoticed as she continued. 'Friday the 23rd five o'clock. He can stay to dinner.' With this order she turned abruptly and left the room. Sally Lane followed out and called to the impervious black-clad back descending the stairs, 'No I shall not . . . ' Her voice trailed off as she caught sight of Charlie just entering the hall. In no fit state to face him at present she turned back and headed for her own room to be alone to think.

Carrying a sprig of viburnum Charlie went straight to Emily Penne's room. The door was still open and before he raised his hand to knock he saw instantly that something was wrong. With an expression of startled surprise the old lady was attempting to sit up in the bed. Her mouth was working but she seemed incapable of speech. As he hurried across to her she fell back exhausted. Weakly she tried to reach out trembling hands to him. Her efforts to speak produced only mumbling sounds which lodged in her throat. Charlie raised her shoulders and adjusted several pillows to support her back. 'All right Emily. It's all right. I'll telephone Doctor Macalistair.'

During her struggles to sit up the hearing aid had fallen out. Charlie picked it up and placed it on the bedside table before going to telephone from the extension in the upstairs corridor.

In her room Sally Lane heard him telephone the doctor and after listening to his first words hurried into Emily Penne's room. Almost on her heels Charlie followed.

'She was perfectly all right just a few minutes ago when I left the room Charlie.'

'Was she asleep then?'

'Yes. I believe so.'

She saw that the old lady was staring fixedly at her. Was it fancy? Or were the eyes accusing? Was it possible that she had been awake? Confusion now prevented clear recollection. The hearing aid on the table caught her attention and she relaxed and at the same time wondered why Martha Oakes had claimed it to be out for repair.

'Get Martha to make a hot drink for Emily,' Charlie ordered.

Shrinking from coming into contact with the housekeeper at present she hurried down to the kitchen and made a pot of tea herself.

Busy unpacking a recently delivered grocery order from a cardboard box Martha Oakes did not speak, presumably having had her say for the time being.

When Sally Lane returned to the bedroom with the tea on a tray she found Emily Penne desperately trying to say something to Charlie, but she was aphasic. At the sound of the doctor's voice down in the hall she put down the tray and went to the head of the stairs.

Martha Oakes who had let him in was unaware of the reason for his re-visit so soon but thought it was to return the hearing aid. She looked surprised when he made his way up the stairs with the words, 'Taken a turn for the worse has she?'

She stood at the base of the stairs and watched as he went into Emily Penne's room.

Moments later, after a quick examination the doctor announced, 'Another stroke I'm afraid. A little more severe this time. All right Emily. Try to relax,' he said as she again struggled unsuccessfully to speak. Noticing the hearing aid on the table he picked it up and placed it in her ear. 'You've been getting yourself excited about something I shouldn't wonder. Now just try to take things easy and we'll have you back on your feet in no time.'

Breathing heavily from exertion Emily Penne lay back against the pillows. For a brief while of indecision the doctor studied her. Still uncertain he said, 'I could have you admitted to hospital but there'd be little they could do except make you comfortable. You're best off here where I know you'd prefer to be. You'll need some professional attention for a while until your condition improves. And with the right attitude and perseverance it will.' He turned to Sally Lane, 'It might prove too much for you alone my dear. I can arrange for a nurse to come in.' He turned now to Charlie. 'What do you think?'

'Lydie has some time off for holiday, two weeks. We had planned that she'd stay here for the whole of that time. She'll be more than willing to take care of Emily. You remember Nurse Collins doctor?'

'I do indeed. A very efficient and capable young lady. I've come across her at times in Nightingale Hospital. But if she's due for holiday then I can tell you she'll be looking forward to the rest from nursing. Rather a busman's holiday otherwise.'

'I know she'll insist on looking after Emily herself,' Charlie assured.

'Don't you think we should at least consult Lydie first?'

'No Doctor. Believe me, I know Lydie. I meant what I said — she will insist.'

'Very well — that's settled then.' The doctor turned back to his patient. 'Now Emily I'm sure you are in complete agreement with these arrangements. Relax as best you can but I want you to continually try to move your limbs to encourage the use back. It will come, but only you can do it. You'll have these young people to help you. You may have difficulty in swallowing for a while so I shall give Martha instructions about your diet. Consommé and any other liquids you fancy is all you'll manage for the time being.' He turned back to Charlie. 'I see they repaired the hearing aid promptly then.'

'Did it while I waited Doctor.'

'Excellent. I must reimburse you since it was I who damaged it.'

'No that won't be necessary.' Charlie waved aside the offer. 'Cost was minimal — so was the damage.'

Doctor Macalistair nodded and seated himself on the bed. 'Now Emily I'm leaving these good people in charge of you. Remember you must keep trying to move your arms and legs. It'll take effort but you must persevere. For the present don't worry too much about speaking. It'll come back. I'll look in again tomorrow morning.'

Emily Penne nodded almost imperceptibly.

As the doctor left the room Charlie and Sally Lane took his place on the bed and each reached out simultaneously for her hands which rested on the counterpane. For a moment or two the old lady looked from one to the other in turn. There was an expression on her face which Sally Lane tried desperately to fathom.

Then Emily Penne's eyes rested on the sprig of viburnum still on the bed where Charlie had dropped it. He picked it up and put it in her palm and tried to fold her hand around it. She gave a weak smile then closed her eyes — as if giving herself up to her impuissance.

In the library Sally Lane dialled the number on a small slip of paper which James Maddison had thrust upon her prior to his departure from the summer house. 'Criterion Hotel. How may I help you?' enquired the articulated speech at the other end of the line.

'I wish to speak with Mr James Maddison please.'

Moments later she heard a click and his voice in her ear. She related the news about Martha Oakes eavesdropping and the consequent threat, and heard him curse loudly. She held the receiver at arms length until his voice had resumed its normal pitch. 'I'll ring the goddamn bitch's neck!'

'Listen,' in the face of his outburst she found it difficult to speak calmly, 'Paula's aunt has had a severe stroke. It happened only today.' She heard his low whistle of surprise.

'Well — what d'you know! How serious? I mean how has it affected her?'

She knew his interest was not the sympathetic kind. 'Her speech has been affected. Now what do I tell . . . ?'

'Leave her to me,' he cut in impatiently. 'I'll take care of the blackmailing old hag. I'll come right away.'

'No don't do that. She said come on Friday the 23rd. We have dinner early on Fridays because she goes to the cinema. Come at five. I'll be waiting to let you in so that we can talk before the others know you've arrived.'

From where she sat at the desk she saw Charlie pass the window. 'Five o'clock sharp,' she ended the call abruptly by replacing the receiver.

Several times during the day Charlie went in to sit with Emily for ten minutes or so. Sally Lane had spent most of the day on the chaise reading aloud to her during the brief intervals when she wasn't dozing. She still wondered at the strange expression in the eyes of the old lady whenever they rested on her. Again she wondered if it was possible that the exchange between herself and Martha Oakes had been overheard and was even perhaps responsible for the stroke.

★   ★   ★

The time was now seven-thirty in the evening. Charlie and Sally Lane had finished dinner. They were seated in Emily Penne's room where, in accord with the doctor's instructions, they had earlier been encouraging her to try to use her paralysed limbs.

Sally Lane had fed consommé to her and

was relieved that, except for a few dribbled spills, this had been managed successfully. Since she was now incapable of speech and no converse with her possible Charlie had spoken of his gardening work for the day and had brought her in another sprig of viburnum.

He had also taken turns at reading aloud to her. All the while he wondered what it was she had so desperately wanted to tell him earlier. He had eventually concluded that it must have been just her distress at the stroke.

'She's asleep now.' Charlie rose from his chair. 'Let's go down and sit in the drawing room for a while. It's warmer down there. We can come up again when she wakes up.'

Sally Lane nodded and followed him downstairs.

'What will you do now that your aunt has taken this latest turn for the worse?'

Charlie poked the logs in the marble fireplace before seating himself in the gentleman's wing-back opposite her.

'I shall of course stay on and hope that she recovers. People do from second strokes I believe. I do hope so.' As she looked across at him the urge to tell him the truth returned. Several times since yesterday she had been on the verge of making the confession. She longed to have him on her side and to feel the masculine comfort of his strong shoulders. But she had been afraid to risk his turning from her in anger. Besides — he wouldn't want her problems inflicted upon him.

'Yes I believe they can recover. Together we'll try to get her back on her feet. Lydie will want to help.'

'Yes — yes of course Charlie. I'll do all I can.'

Since discovering Emily Penne's seizure was so serious he had thought long and deep. There was every possibility that she was close to death despite their efforts to help her recover. There was little or no hope now that she could make any changes to her will in his favour regarding the house; although he still didn't know what that registered letter from her solicitor contained. He desperately wanted to stay on at Grandstone House, preferably as its master. But there would be little hope of that if the will was already in the niece's favour as far as the house was concerned. Unless she would agree to marry him. He was well and truly settled in and wanted to stay that way. The garden had flourished in his care; never in his life had he felt so content as when working in it.

His eyes rested on her. The vast room was presently lit by a brass standard lamp and the glow from the firelight. She looked very attractive but he knew that he did not love her in the accepted sense of a lover's feelings. She was pleasant company. Even though not as self-assured as he would have expected. On the contrary she struck him as being particularly unpretentious, almost diffident to Emily Penne, and at times seemed totally preoccupied.

To start over elsewhere would never be the same, and he could not possibly expect to strike so lucky again. He considered that he had given the old lady value for money in attention, devotion to duty, and time; more than her niece had given her in the past until now. There seemed only one certain way of possessing Grandstone House. If he waited for the reading of the will, which might not happen for years despite the old lady's present state of health, the girl might meanwhile have married someone else.

Still . . . he could wait a little longer before taking such a serious step. In any case he couldn't be sure that she would accept him. Never had he shown the slightest interest in her romantically. She would understand his love of the old house though and know it to be the reason behind a marriage proposal if he made one.

No, for the moment he would do nothing, say nothing on the subject. Just wait awhile.

Perhaps Emily might confide in him on matters concerning her will if she recovered her speech.

★ ★ ★

When Charlie had telephoned Lydie with the news of Emily Penne's stroke and explained its severity she had wanted to go to Grandstone House immediately. But this she was unable to do since there was not enough warning to arrange an instant change of shift or relief of duty. The stroke had happened on Thursday, only two days before her expected weekend visit.

Charlie arrived early on Saturday morning to collect her from the nurses' quarters.

When they arrived at the house Lydie went straight to Emily Penne's bedroom and immediately took over the care of her at least for the weekend. This gave Sally Lane a break.

'Now Emily,' Lydie was saying, 'I aim to get you back on your feet, but you'll have to cooperate. Is that understood?'

Affection shone in the eyes of the old lady as she nodded in response.

Lydie smiled and kissed the pale cheek. Then losing no time she set about the task of massage therapy. At the same time she instructed Sally Lane in the procedure so that she could continue with this in her absence.

During the morning Clive Wessley telephoned to say that he could manage a few hours off-duty the next day and that he would arrive as early as possible on Sunday morning. He had taken Lydie out to dinner the previous evening and been given the news about the stroke. 'We'll get a nurse in to help and give you a break during the Christmas holiday,' he said. 'I know Emily well and am absolutely certain that she'd agree with me on that.'

'Yes I know that too Clive but I want to take care of her myself whenever I can. Remember I have help here anyway — there are three of us besides Charlie.'

'I'm aware of that but you still need a break after working at the hospital all week. I want to see something of you too. I'll be taking a few days break myself.'

'Yes I know and I'll be spending some of it with you. We'll plan it tomorrow when you arrive. Bye for now Clive.' Lydie replaced the receiver and returned to Emily Penne's room. Of course Christmas arrangements must go ahead as planned, but it wouldn't be the carefree event that they'd envisaged when making them. If they all sat around subdued, without making some effort to celebrate, it would have a more depressing effect on Emily herself. Lydie knew her well enough by now to be sure of this. She'd remarked often that she enjoyed their bright company around her at the weekends. She was more in need of it now than even before. Lydie did not in the least begrudge the time she would spend in nursing her. Emily had shown great kindness and genuine affection, offering unstinting hospitality at all times and had always given a warm welcome. Many weekends now Lydie had spent at the house since that first visit. She even kept most of her clothes in the wardrobe of the bedroom that was always referred to as hers and which she had been allowed to choose for herself on her first weekend stay.

15

Earlier in the week Charlie had gone into town to order the best available wheelchair to provide some mobility for Emily Penne. This had been delivered and he had carried her downstairs to the drawing room. She was now seated in the wheelchair close to the window.

He, Lydie, and Sally Lane had persevered in their efforts to encourage her to try to regain the use of her limbs. So far there had been little or no improvement.

'How's that? Comfortable?' Charlie adjusted the rug across her knees.

She nodded and looked at him with that same anxious, almost pleading, expression that he'd seen in her eyes every day since the stroke a week ago. It had gradually become clear to him that she was trying to communicate something important, for at times she became quite agitated. Charlie felt inadequate and helpless in his attempts to understand what it was she wanted to tell him. All manner of questions he had asked and watched closely for some change in her eyes that would tell him he had asked the

207

right one. He talked a great deal about the garden so that she wouldn't feel so cut off from the daily activity out there. But his efforts seemed to add to her frustration.

'Well at least you're mobile now that we have the chair. I can take you outside. Today mightn't be a good idea though. It's very cold.' He set about showing her how to operate the movement of the chair, but her hands could not at present cope with the action. 'It'll come. We must be patient. I'm just going into the garden for a minute. I'll be straight back.'

He returned carrying a sprig of viburnum which he placed in her lap. 'Try to grasp it. Come on — try,' he coaxed.

There was a faint flicker of movement in her fingers as she strove to obey, and he knew that her determination was wrestling with the affliction. The effort brought tears to her eyes.

'Good.' He patted her hand encouragingly. 'You're improving already. Keep trying.'

Sally Lane entered the room carrying a book from which she would read aloud to Emily as this was the most comfortable one-sided communication at present. Too much talking to which the old lady was unable to respond only caused her more frustration. Besides which small chat, casual remarks and comments to a mute listener were soon exhausted.

She seated herself on the window seat close to the wheelchair.

When she saw the trembling fingers attempting to curl around the sprig of a viburnum tears sprang to her own eyes. 'Good. That's wonderful. Your fingers definitely moved Emily.' She put aside the book and proceeded with the massaging therapy in the way that Lydie had instructed. This therapy she carried out several times a day. 'Did you see that movement Charlie?'

'I did.' Charlie gave a smile of encouragement and approval. 'Keep it up, Emily. Now I'm just going into the village to pick up a Christmas tree, must have a tree in the hall. By the time I get back I hope to see you holding that sprig properly.' He inclined his head and winked at her. 'I shan't be gone long.' He had decided that the previous arrangements for the Christmas season should go ahead as planned. Both Lydie and Sally Lane had been in agreement on this.

* * *

As Charlie drove along Berry Lane his thoughts dwelt on the girl to whom he had considered proposing marriage. They had spent a few evenings together at the theatre, and he had shown her a little of London; but romance had never been a component of those times together. Their outings had been merely social companionship. He definitely did not harbour any romantic feelings for her. But they could, if married, maintain and preserve Grandstone House together, and for the present this was the paramount consideration.

He did wonder however just what the relationship was between her and the American chap whom she had apparently invited to dine with them on Friday. He also wondered why the old lady had become so agitated when told of the arrangement. In fact he had interpreted the expression on her face as alarm. It was possible, even probable, that her brain had been affected by the recent stroke. Still engrossed in speculation he drew up outside the greengrocer shop and went in to inspect the collection of Christmas trees on display just inside the entrance. The faces of the two teenage assistants brightened up as both went to assist him.

★ ★ ★

Nights had been sleepless for Sally Lane for the past week. Incessantly her thoughts dwelt on the coming meeting between Martha

Oakes and James Maddison. No way could she figure that he would allow the house-keeper to outwit or hold a trump card against him, or be compliant with her terms of silence. Many times in the past she had seen him do battle with tough businessmen successfully. But this situation was somewhat different. How could he outmanoeuvre Martha Oakes's tongue except by succumbing to her demands.

In her present state of mind Sally Lane was unable to properly consider the situation of blackmail that she was facing in relation to its effect on any legacy left to Charlie. At worse she could give the two vultures the share of the inheritance which they were demanding and then make the rest over to him. Yet what reason could she give him for handing over more than two-thirds of the estate to them? As far as Martha Oakes was concerned she could claim that she considered the house-keeper deserved more than a cottage on account of her long and loyal service at Grandstone House. To explain away the share she was giving to James Maddison . . . perhaps she could claim that she was in debt to his company. There was no way in which she could dispose of any part of the estate without Charlie's knowledge. Since he handled all the financial business of the household and had access to all bank statements he would know the exact extent of the Penneston-Barkley assets.

On her way down to the drawing room she reflected again on the alternative course open to her. *Confession*. But, apart from the harm this would do mentally and physically to Emily, she feared the consequences for her own sake. She had no idea of what the penalty was for impersonating another person for gain. With James Maddison against her no one would believe the true facts of the matter now that Paula was no longer here to corroborate the truth.

She was half-way down the stairs when she remembered the letter. Suddenly weak from relief she stopped and promptly sat down. Two weeks after her arrival at the house she had written Paula a letter addressed to her apartment. The contents of that letter would at least be proof that she was here at Paula's request and knowledge. Where was that letter? It had never been returned undelivered. Could it be that James Maddison had taken charge of it — perhaps had it in his possession still? No, more likely he would have destroyed it as obsolete. With this thought her hopes faded and left only disappointment. It stood to reason that he would have destroyed it to protect himself.

The letter had been signed in her own name which he had claimed to the authorities was that of the murder victim.

Briefly the futile thought flashed through her mind of how very different everything would be right now if Paula had come on this visit. The biggest difference . . . she would still be alive. She would have been here in this lovely old house with her aunt and Charlie. Would she have fallen in love with him and stayed? She doubted it. Paula had been a dominant personality who needed a dominant man. Charlie was such a gentleman; quite the reverse of James Maddison who, to her present way of thinking, was the personification of the Devil himself, totally evil. A shiver passed through her at the thought of the headstone that bore her name somewhere in a New York cemetery.

She rose from the stair and continued on down.

★ ★ ★

Clive Wessley had been unable to officially go off-duty in time to collect Lydie and drive her to Grandstone House for the start of her Christmas leave from the hospital. Since she was anxious to arrive as soon as possible she caught the train to the city station where it had been arranged that Charlie would pick her up in the Bentley.

Now, seated beside him, she explained the plans she had made for later that day.

'Clive's going to call in on his way home to collect me and take me to his home for dinner. I hope Emily won't mind my being absent just for the once. They've arranged for an early dinner because his parents are going out to visit friends afterwards. I should be back by around ten-thirty tonight.'

'Well it so happens that we have a visitor coming to dinner this evening. An American a guest of our guest so to speak.'

'Really! I hope they won't take it amiss then — my not being present.'

'Of course not — why should they. We don't know him. Chap she works for in New York. I suppose I should use the past tense since she's not planning to go back there.'

'I'm surprised they chose this evening. Martha Oakes goes to the cinema on Friday evenings. She always serves dinner earlier specially.'

'Well maybe she's going to give it a miss this week being so close to Christmas. I know that she's planning to spend Christmas day with her sister in the village. But I expect you already know that piece of good news.'

'Yes. Emily mentioned it to me a while

back. Martha prepares everything in advance for Christmas dinner before she goes off. It's been her usual practice for years apparently. It's of no consequence whether or not she prepares the meal beforehand. I'd enjoy doing it all myself. Of course things can't be as we planned before Emily's stroke.'

'No. It must be pretty hard for her being unable to communicate. There's something important she's been trying to tell me. I'm sure of it. I've tried to make guesses but haven't hit upon the right thing yet.' Charlie stopped the car at traffic lights.

'Oh I dare say it's just general frustration. It's very distressing for her. Has she made any progress this week?'

'Very slightly, but definitely. We haven't let up on the massage therapy and encouraging her to help herself.' The lights turned green and the car moved off. 'What time is Wessley picking you up?'

'He should arrive about five. Depending on what time he gets away.' She was always secretly amused that Charlie would only refer to Clive by his surname except when in his company. Obviously he still had reservations about him. Perhaps some psychological element was involved on account that he was a detective.

'Well I expect you'll have left the house

before the American visitor arrives. I'm wondering what he came to England for.'

'Business no doubt. He probably knows by now that she's decided not to go back there.'

'Yes no doubt,' Charlie agreed. 'I heard from our Ron yesterday. He's been accepted as a migrant to Australia on the ten pound fare scheme.'

'That's wonderful news Charlie. Has a date been set?'

'Yes, sails on the 4th of February. The fact that Fred's offering him a home and can set him up in a job helped apparently. It means that he won't be a liability to the government over there. That and his age speeded up the process. He's looking forward to going. I shall be paying his fare of course. Poor little sod wouldn't be able to raise the ten pounds himself, although he has been trying to save up for it.'

'We must give him a party and we'll see him off at the docks.'

'Sure thing Lyd. We'll take him out to dinner at that last hotel where I worked and shopping to get some clothes. He's bound to need some new gear to take with him.'

'Then all of you will have left home. Your mum will be on her own.'

'No not her. She's thinking of taking in a lodger Ron says. Already got him lined up shouldn't wonder. Someone she's met in the pub no doubt. I must pop in and see her one of these days.'

As they drove in through the high wide wrought-iron gates with the name of the house worked into the metal Lydie sighed. 'Ah — it's good to come home to this lovely old place. It's so restful. Ron's never seen it has he. You must bring him here before he leaves England.'

'I intended to. He wants to see the house before he goes. If it hadn't been for Emily's stroke I'd have arranged for him to spend Christmas here. It'll almost certainly be his last in England.'

'He may come back to visit.'

'I doubt it. Fred never has.'

'Well there's still time for that Charlie.'

Charlie dropped her off at the front entrance and drove the Bentley into the garage.

* * *

Clive Wessley parked his car outside the small police station attached to the house where George Hill lived alone. How good it always felt when he reached Redcliffe village knowing that home was only minutes away. He entered the tiny office and greeted the police sergeant heartily. 'Hello George. Just called in to wish you a Merry Christmas.'

'Hello Clive. Free for the holiday season then I see. Have a good one and forget about crime for a few days. Easier said than done I know. Home's the best place. Will you be calling in at Grandstone House as usual on Christmas day?'

'Shall do George, but not to stay for long. It'd be too much for Emily under the circumstances. You will have heard about her recent stroke of course.'

'No I haven't! When did — ?'

'Just over a week ago now. Pretty serious this time.'

'I'm surprised that Martha didn't call in and let me know! She comes into the village often enough. I haven't seen her since she dropped in to show me a newspaper cutting claiming that it was a photo of the chap who works for Emily now. Charlie something.'

Clive Wessley looked amused. 'Funny old stick Martha Oakes. Never could fathom her. Too quiet. Always seems to have a resentful expression on her face. Don't know how Emily has tolerated her all these years with that depressing aura about her. What was her problem then?'

George Hill explained, then added, 'I did telephone Emily a day or so afterwards to tell her of Martha's visit and the reason. She as good as told me to mind my own business.'

'I'm not surprised under the circumstances.'

'Me neither. But I did it to satisfy Martha. I hadn't seen Charlie then so have no idea if there was some likeness or not. Seen him since though. Fine looking chap. Certainly looks straight enough. Although I did do a little checking up just to appease Martha. Even though I know she's a peculiar old bird. Found out that the chappie in the newspaper photo had been released from a six month jail term back in April . . . oh it's not worth relating.'

'Well I'm glad you did check otherwise she'd have been on to me to. Now I must be off. I'm calling in on Emily on my way home and hoping there's some improvement in her condition. This stroke completely paralysed her and she can't speak.'

'As serious as that! I really had no idea. I'm truly sorry to hear it. I usually call in to wish her a Merry Christmas. Have done for years now. I'll check with Doctor Macalistair first though to see if she can have visitors. Loss of speech must be devastating on top of losing the use of limbs.'

'Damn right it must. In any case feel free to

drop in at Tanglewood for a drink as usual George.'

'Thanks Clive, will do. Give my best wishes to John and Mary. Tell Emily I'll pop in if the doc gives the okay.'

'Will do George. So long now.'

16

For the sixth time in the last five minutes James Maddison glanced at his watch. He frowned and poured himself another whisky. 'What the hell,' he muttered irritably; why should he time his arrival to the exact minute! He was impatient to get the measure of the Oakes bitch. He intended to settle her once and for all. No old hag was going to call the tune for him.

He threw back his head and tossed down the spirits. Then he picked up a small brown bottle from the table. Absently he stared at the printed label bearing the name of his late wife. These were the sleeping pills that had been found in the pocket of the coat she'd been wearing at the time of her accident, and returned to him by the police. He tipped out the pills into a pocket in his jacket. They would come in handy after all and he was glad he hadn't disposed of them. He went to fetch his top-coat.

Ten minutes short of the arranged time he drove his hired car through the entrance gates of Grandstone House.

Seated on a leather couch in the library

Sally Lane toyed nervously with the fine cashmere scarf at her neck as she waited for the dreaded arrival of James Maddison. She was trembling slightly from fear or cold, perhaps both, she wasn't sure.

She had felt relieved when Lydie and Clive Wessley left to go to his home. She had been on edge all the while they were in the house, willing them to be gone before the visitor arrived. She had contrived to get Charlie to drive into town for a few items of last-minute Christmas shopping, on the pretext that these had been overlooked. She had timed the request so that he'd be away from the house at five o'clock when James Maddison was due to arrive. He was unaware of the arranged meeting with Martha Oakes. By the time he returned it would be over and she would know the worse.

During the nerve-racking wait over the last few days she had avoided the housekeeper as much as was possible. Power and threat seemed to exude from her stiff silent figure as she moved about the house.

At present Emily Penne was dozing in the wheelchair by the drawing room fire. Reading aloud to her had offered some respite and helped to pass the time without the mentally exhausting necessity of keeping up one-sided dialogue. It had also served to stem the desperate mumbling that appeared to wear her out. It was impossible to know what was going on in her mind behind that strange stark expression; or even if she was paying any attention to the reading.

A car drew up outside. As it was not yet the appointed time for James Maddison she feared that Charlie had returned, even though unlikely so soon. She went to the window to investigate but could see no one. Before she could make any further move the library door was opened. James Maddison entered followed by Martha Oakes who had been watching out for his arrival and had let him in by a side entrance.

17

Martha Oakes glanced at the kitchen clock as she removed her apron. She was running a few minutes late despite having, as was usual on Fridays, served the dinner early in order to catch the beginning of the film and last house at the town cinema.

Well satisfied with the way her arranged meeting with the American had gone, even better than she'd hoped for, her thin lips slid briefly into an oblique half-smile of victory. He had been a pushover. She was still feeling surprised at that because he didn't strike her as the sort to whom one could dictate terms. She wasn't too happy that he was still in the house and at present in the drawing room with Charlie, Sally Lane, and Emily Penne. The doors were closed to keep in the warmth from the log fire.

Dressed in her best black coat and wearing an extra cardigan as insulation against the cold evening which would turn to a frosty night she opened the drawing room doors and announced to no one in particular, 'I've filled the log-box it's outside the back door.' She closed the door and went out through a side-entrance to collect her bicycle from the garage.

At this point James Maddison excused himself to go to the cloakroom. From a window he watched her mount the bicycle and as she rode off wondered vaguely how she managed to avoid getting the long coat caught up in the wheels. Dismissing the idle thought he fingered the loose pills in his jacket pocket and returned to the drawing-room.

Before she reached the end of the drive Martha Oakes noticed that the front tyre of the bicycle was flat. Only that morning she had pumped it up on her return from the village. To do so again now would be futile since it obviously required a patch. 'Bugger,' she muttered, annoyed at this further delay as she returned the bicycle to the garage. She slipped back into the house by the same side-door and telephoned for a taxi. Although not usually given to using taxicabs she knew Ted Gilbert's number by heart, since she passed the notice in his window every time she visited her sister in the village.

As she left the house again she wondered why the American was still hanging about where he was not welcome. Having decided to start walking along the lane where Ted Gilbert could pick her up she strode briskly along the driveway. At least this would save some time and was preferable to waiting about in the cold for his arrival. Even with this delay she would still be in time for the last house, since the journey along the lane would be quicker by car. In any case the bus driver would surely hang on for a few minutes. He knew that she always caught his bus into town every Friday evening. It would be necessary to call in on Mary to let her know about the puncture and that she wouldn't be leaving the bike as she usually did when catching the bus. She could borrow Mary's bike to get home. Couldn't expect Ted Gilbert to stay up until that time of night just to drive her back to the house.

In the lane she shone the small torch that she always carried with her on cinema nights. It came in useful to show the way to her seat. Those usherettes gave only a quick flash of their torches and left people to find their own way in the dark.

Ted Gilbert drew up alongside and she got into the car. As he turned at a field-gate he said, 'No bike tonight Martha? Do you want me to meet the bus to drive you home?' He knew her habit of leaving her bicycle at her sister's house and collecting it when she got off the bus.

'No need thank you. I shall borrow Mary's

bike to ride back.'

'Means that you'll have to return it to her sometime though and a walk home from the village.'

'That doesn't bother me in the daytime.'

He dropped her off at her sister's cottage and she paid him. 'If you change your mind Martha just knock on my door. I'll be up late tonight hanging decorations and preparing for Christmas visitors.'

Some hopes she thought as she opened the cottage gate. No call to go spending money. Time enough for that when . . . And the signs were that it wouldn't be too long in coming. Have more than she knew what to do with then. It had all been so easy. To her great surprise the American had offered no resistance. She had expected some however futile it would have been for him.

A little later she arrived at the bus stop just as the bus was pulling in.

She felt in good humour, a feeling alien to her nature, when fifteen minutes later she flashed her torch and made her way to her seat in the cinema.

★   ★   ★

In the drawing room Charlie drew the wheelchair closer to the fire. During the

227

course of the evening he had at various times asked Emily Penne if she wished to be taken up to her room. By a vigorous shaking of her head she had replied.

Lydie was still at Tanglewood with Clive Wessley and was not expected back for some while yet. She had been gone less than two hours.

He wondered when the American would leave. At present he was showing no signs of doing so. Charlie did not like him. There was something about him he could not take to, something he couldn't quite fathom. When he'd been introduced to Emily Penne by Sally Lane, who had explained that he had been her employer back in New York, the old lady had become extremely agitated and only with the utmost difficulty had Charlie managed to calm her. It appeared as if she was struggling to make some protest at the visitor's presence. Charlie had become convinced that the stroke had affected her brain after all. He was impatient to see the visitor leave and hoped this would be the last they would see of him. He hadn't mentioned where he planned to spend Christmas and certainly seemed the kind who would invite himself to the house again. He decided to ask outright. 'Are you intending to return to

New York for Christmas?'

'No. I have some business to attend to in London. I shall stay over at my hotel.' James Maddison glanced at his watch as he answered.

Charlie had noticed that he'd been doing this incessantly during the last half-hour or so and concluded that the American had some appointment to keep later in the evening.

Although James Maddison kept up some sort of conversational small-talk Charlie sensed that his mind was preoccupied.

At nine-thirty, after another quick glance at his watch, James Maddison announced, 'I guess I should be going but I sure could use some coffee before I leave.'

Relieved that he was at last making a move to go Sally Lane jumped up instantly to offer. 'I'll make some for all of us.'

'Would you like another brandy with it,' Charlie asked, more to ease what seemed a tense atmosphere than for reasons of hospitality. He felt sure that the American's presence disturbed the old lady. Also he thought that the chap had already drunk enough spirits, even though he seemed well able to handle the drink.

'No thanks, coffee will be just fine.'

Shortly Sally Lane returned with a tray

bearing four cups of coffee already poured, sugar and a jug of cream.

As she entered the room James Maddison sprang from his chair and took the tray from her. 'I'll serve.'

With faint surprise she relinquished the tray and watched as he set it down on a side table furthest from where she and Charlie were seated.

'Now does everyone take sugar and cream?'. As he spoke he turned so that his right hand was hidden from their view.

'Yes please,' Sally Lane replied for them all.

He took from his pocket some of the loose sleeping pills and dropped two into each of the three cups. He was completely unconcerned that the wheelchair was placed in direct line of vision to his actions and that its occupant was looking his way. He threw a quick glance in that direction and saw that the eyes of Emily Penne were fixed intently upon him, just as they had been all evening. But he didn't care. Since she could not speak she posed no threat.

He left his own coffee on the table and took the tray across to hand round the cups. Sally Lane took one and Charlie took the remaining two, one of which he placed on the coffee table close to the wheelchair. He would assist Emily with it when it had cooled sufficiently. As he did this she started her desperate mumblings again, shaking her head from side to side frantically, at the same time her eyes trying to indicate the coffee. He knew that she was trying to tell him something about it. 'All right Emily. Don't distress yourself if you don't want it.'

Tears of frustration now filled her eyes and she made a renewed effort to make him understand. If only he would ask the right questions so that she could save him from the menacing stranger in the room. Ceaselessly she attempted to impel life into her hands. Her useless fingers twitched and trembled pathetically as her brain tried to compel them to obey, to move and knock the coffee cup off the table as a sign to him not to drink it. But Charlie returned to his seat and started to drink hoping this might hasten the departure of their unwanted guest. With a sob of helplessness Emily Penne watched him.

Sally Lane who had picked up her own coffee and was about to drink paused and put it down. She too was concerned by the old lady's obvious distress. She crossed to the wheelchair and patted the agitated hand in attempt to calm her. 'Don't upset yourself Emily. Would you like to go up to your room?'

Emily Penne tried again, looking first at the coffee to indicate it and then at the one in

Charlie's hand, at the same time shaking her head, her eyes imploring. Then she looked back at James Maddison. An expression of fear showed on her face now.

Unperturbed he placed his half finished coffee back on the tray and said, 'Well I must be off. I can manage to see myself out. You folks stay in the warm. Good-night.' He glanced at Charlie who made an unsuccessful attempt to get up.

With satisfaction James Maddison noted the empty cup. The coffee was drunk. That was the main thing for the present, as long as the Lydie girl they'd mentioned did not show up just yet. He threw a glance at Sally Lane who was still beside the wheelchair attempting to calm its occupant.

'Don't let your coffee get cold,' he said and went out closing the drawing room door behind him before she could respond.

In the hall he snatched his top-coat from the stand and let himself out of the house.

In the drawing room Sally Lane stared at the closed door hardly daring to trust that he really had left, and at the same time wondered why he had stayed so long. In no mood herself for his unwanted company at dinner she had spoken very little and had noticed that Charlie had done his best to be polite and sociable. She sensed that he had not taken to the guest. She'd noted too how disturbed Emily had been by his presence. She returned to her seat and was about to pick up her coffee again when the desperate mumbling became louder than before. She could not calmly sit drinking while the old lady was looking so distraught. Fearing for her condition she put the cup down again and went back to sit beside the wheelchair. 'It's all right Emily.' She had dropped the title of Aunt only days after arriving at Grandstone House since it had seemed less deceitful to refer to her by name only. 'He's gone now. I know you didn't like him. Neither do I. But don't worry. I promise I shall never allow him to come here again. Lydie should be home soon.' She was aware that Emily was very fond of Lydie. But Lydie had earned that affection, as Charlie had. As for herself . . . she had been handicapped from the very beginning by her own conscience, however well-meaning her intentions had been.

Emily Penne fixed stark eyes on Charlie in the large wing-back chair. Seeing the fear there Sally Lane turned to glance at him. She showed surprise on seeing that he'd fallen asleep, his head slumped forward onto his chest. She had been so busy trying to calm

Emily that she hadn't noticed. 'Charlie,' she called.

When there was no response she crossed to the wing-back and shook his arm. 'Wake up Charlie I need your help.' She shook him more roughly now by his shoulders, which was no easy task. His eyes remained closed and his dead weight fell back in the chair.

Emily Penne continued her desperate efforts to speak. Sally Lane glanced across at her and saw that she had managed to raise her right hand slightly, her eyes concentrated on the door to which she was willing her unresponsive arm to lift and point. In an attempt to calm her Sally Lane went across to the door, which was not quite closed. Before closing it she glanced out to ensure that the visitor really had left. The front door was still open. She concluded that the latch had not caught sufficiently to secure it and the draught had blown it half-open. She shivered as a blast of cold air struck her on the way across the hall. About to close the door an impulse struck her to glance outside. At first all seemed intensely black. For a moment or two she stood staring out while her eyes adjusted to the darkness. With surprise she saw the dark outline of a car parked close to the hedge. It could not be the Bentley because Charlie always garaged it after use and in any event would certainly not have left it out exposed to the frost. Perplexed she stood considering the possibility that James Maddison was still in the house since the car must be the hired one in which he had arrived. She stepped back inside to check the coat-stand in the hall. His coat was not there. She went outside to inspect the car. Her eyes had adjusted to the darkness. A silver key-ring glowed softly in the reflected light from the front porch. The keys were in the ignition. 'James?' she called softly and glanced about her. Then she saw the faint outline of the open garage doors. Of course — Martha Oakes was not yet home. The doors were always left open on Fridays for her to return her bicycle. Some instinct urged her towards it. She gave a gasp of surprise when she saw that the car was not there. Why would James Maddison take the Bentley and leave behind the hired car? A possible answer suggested itself. Perhaps he had run out of petrol. As she was about to turn away the faint glow of a shiny object caught her eye. She groped for one of the flash-lights that hung on a wall of the garage, kept there for the use of the last person to come from the garage after dark. In the beam of the torch she saw that the object was the bell of Martha Oakes's old upright bicycle which stood against a wall. Martha must already be home from the movies. 'Strange I never heard her come in,' she said aloud. Must have been before James Maddison had left or the front door would not be open. The beam picked out the badly deflated tyre. Puzzled she returned to the hired car. He should have at least asked permission to take the Bentley, damn nerve he had! How on earth did he intend to return it? Things weren't making sense! She checked the fuel gauge of the car and saw that the tank was still three quarters full. She sat in the driving seat and switched on the ignition. The engine purred smoothly at first touch despite the cold. Completely baffled she got from the car and stood for a few moments thinking and hugging herself against the bitterly cold air. What possible reason would he have for taking the Bentley and leaving the hired car behind? She went back into the house to check that Martha Oakes had returned. When a search failed to find her a sudden fear struck her for the safety of the housekeeper and she went back outside. Uncharacteristically James Maddison had been altogether too easy with her terms of silence. At the time she had thought it strange and unlike him not to quibble. He had been meekly compliant, even if Martha Oakes did wield a sinister power such as he'd never had to contend with before. Her tongue was her weapon. It could send him to gaol. Under these conditions he might well stop at nothing to silence her. Yet this did not answer why he had taken the Bentley. Shivering she listened for the sound of a car in the lane. Only the call of an owl broke the frosty silence.

★   ★   ★

In the lane James Maddison turned the Bentley to face in the direction of the house, parked it close to the hedge, then switched off the headlamps. In the darkness he sat alert, waiting. According to information gleaned from Sally Lane, Martha Oakes should be along at any moment now. He had been told of her habit of collecting her bicycle from her sister's cottage and riding home from the village after being dropped off from the bus. In advance of his visit he had checked the times of the last bus into Redcliffe village. All was silent except for the impatient drumming of his gloved fingers on the steering wheel. He glanced again at the illuminated dial of his watch. She should be along at any time now. Eyes intent on the driving mirror he waited, alert and ready for action. Then, reflected in the mirror, he saw a thin wavering light moving towards the car in the darkness.

A malicious glint lit his eyes. He swung round in his seat and waited until he could pick out the outline of the long old-fashioned coat.

Ready for action he faced the front again and switched on the ignition, his eyes riveted on the approaching light in the mirror.

On the borrowed bicycle Martha Oakes was within ten yards of the parked car when she made out the dark outline and heard the soft purr of the engine. Suspicious she stopped pedalling and dismounted. Although not generally of a nervous disposition she decided that there was no sense in taking chances. The car must have parked for no good purpose since its lights were switched off and the engine running. She turned and pushed the bicycle back along the lane to a field-gate which was the only break in the hedge for some distance. Every step, every bush and tree along the lane she knew well, even in the dark. Ears straining she stood still and listened. The car engine was suddenly switched off. A moment later she heard the sound of the door closing and footsteps coming towards her. Then a powerful flashlight threw its beam along the lane in her direction.

An old oak-tree, famous for its huge dimensions, stood further into the field. She opened the gate just enough to slip through with the bicycle and closed it behind her hoping the sound did not carry. Then she made for the oak and gained its cover just as the glow of the torch-light lit up the five-bar gate. The footsteps halted and the dancing beam of light paused — like a cat about to spring. She pressed herself and the bicycle closer to the old tree-trunk.

★   ★   ★

Misgivings mounting Sally Lane went back into the house and into the drawing room. With desperate urgency she attempted to rouse Charlie. She called his name and slapped his face lightly, to no avail. She caught sight of his empty cup and her gaze shifted to her own untouched drink. Suspicions further aroused she connected his almost unconscious state with the coffee, recalling that James Maddison had made it his business to serve it. She glanced across to the table where he had set the tray down after taking it from her. She became aware that Emily Penne was still continuing her mumblings. Realisation struck her that from the position of the wheelchair in relation to the table where he had stood it would have been possible for Emily to have seen him putting the sugar and cream or anything else into the cups. Had she been looking that way? Perhaps, for she had barely taken her eyes from him all evening.

During these last concerned minutes she had been half ignoring the background mumblings. Now she crossed to the wheelchair. 'The coffee! Did you see — ?'

She spoke the words as both question and answer and saw the relief in the eyes of Emily Penne who was nodding frantically in reply. She also saw the fear, and leaned closer to speak more clearly and distinctly despite the hearing aid. 'Did Martha say if she was staying at her sister's house overnight? She hasn't taken her bicycle with her and she should be home by now if she took a cab?'

Emily Penne shook her head.

Convinced now that James Maddison had some sinister motive in taking the Bentley her fears for the safety of Martha Oakes increased. She continued, 'I must go and look for her. When I get back I'll try to explain a few things to you and Charlie. Now try not to worry. Everything will be okay.' She turned towards the door but before reaching it an idea occurred to her. She remembered seeing a small bottle of smelling-salts on the dressing table in Emily's bedroom, and wondered if these might revive Charlie.

Not since a small child had she come

across the old fashioned remedy which in bygone days had been used to revive fainting ladies. She could recall quite clearly a time when as a child she had picked up a tiny fancy-shaped bottle of pretty pastel crystals and opened the top. She had taken a good sniff at the contents and been almost knocked off her feet. Her nose had stung badly and her eyes had smarted and watered.

All this went through her mind as she raced up the stairs, stumbling on the way in her haste. In the bedroom she went across to the place where she had seen the bottle. It wasn't there. She made a hasty but unsuccessful search. In a state of near-panic she did not waste any more precious time and ran back downstairs. She needed Charlie's help to deal with James Maddison who was a strong man. Alone she would be helpless to stop him if he was intent on harming Martha Oakes. On the bottom stair she missed her footing, stumbled and wrenched her ankle. As she got up she winced as she put weight on the injured foot. Limping now she returned to the drawing room to check if Charlie had woken. He was still in the same position as when she'd left him moments ago. 'I'm going to telephone Clive,' she called across to Emily Penne. Limping she left the room, oblivious to the pain in her ankle.

On the pad beside the telephone on the hall-table the Wessley's telephone number was at the top of the list. With trembling hands she picked up the receiver and dialled.

* * *

In Tanglewood Clive Wessley predicted, 'It's going to be a freezer tonight. I'm just going to slip out to the stables and cover the horses.'

'I'll come with you to help,' Lydie offered. 'I'll just get my coat.'

Arms about each other they went out into the grounds of the old country house. It was while they were outside that Sally Lane telephoned. But the stables were out of earshot of the phone. It was still ringing as they came within hearing range on their return.

'Listen! I think I hear the phone.' Clive Wessley took Lydie by the hand and together they raced towards the house. Just as they re-entered by the back entrance the ringing ceased. 'Blast! Just missed it. Never mind they'll ring back. Most likely Mum and Dad to say they'll be late home.'

'I'd best stay only for another half-hour Clive. I was expected back almost an hour ago. Not that they'll mind of course but with Emily in such a bad way and it being my first day home ... Strange that I think of Grandstone House as home now.'

'This will be your home soon Lydie; although you haven't yet decided when.'

'Well I shall have to wait until Emily has recovered a little before I can break the news to her.'

'Yes of course. But as it's good news I shouldn't think it would do her much harm to be told soon.'

'Probably not. We'll discuss it some more with your parents and get their opinion about that.'

They seated themselves in front of the drawing room log-fire. 'That call Clive — it might have been your chief super, but I hope not.'

'I certainly hope not too. I want a nice quiet three days with you, so let's trust that the lesser civilised out there behave themselves for the next seventy two hours at least.'

★ ★ ★

When her call went unanswered after prolonged ringing Sally Lane had to assume there was no one home at Tanglewood. It might also mean that Lydie and Clive were on their way, bringing Lydie back to the house. But she could not be certain and valuable time was passing. Every moment might count and Martha Oakes would by now be in the lane on her way home. Out in the hall she glanced at the cloak-stand. Her own coat was upstairs in her wardrobe. No time to fetch it, especially with the added handicap of her injured ankle. She snatched Martha's old-fashioned black coat from the peg and limped out of the front door not stopping to close it behind her. On the way to the garage she struggled into the cumbersome coat that reached to her ankles. As she passed the hired car she threw a cursory glance at it, regretting that she hadn't yet learned to drive and vowing to do so at the earliest opportunity now. Perhaps Charlie would teach her.

In the garage she grasped the old upright, mounted it with difficulty, and headed along the driveway. Several times on the way she lost her balance, hampered by the long coat, added to which her painful ankle and the flat tyre made it difficult to stay balanced. She wondered if it would save time in the long run if she stopped to inflate the tyre. But concluded that if this were possible Martha Oakes would have done so herself. She also tried to judge whether it might be quicker on foot. Again she decided against on account of her injured ankle. The high saddle added to the difficulty in handling the bicycle under the adverse conditions and she became dismounted several times. At the gate she turned right into the lane.

★   ★   ★

Martha Oakes heard the crunch of feet on frozen earth and leaves as he entered the field-gate. For a moment the probing flashlight swung close to her hiding place. She stood stock-still. Any snapping of a twig under her feet or the wheel of the bicycle would sound like the crack of a whip in the silence.

The light-ray glided and wavered as it sought her out, first along the hedge, then slowly moved across the field. As the old oak came under the spotlight she held her breath and pressed herself closer to the trunk. She heard footfalls on the rough dirt-path that bordered the field. For a moment the beam highlighted the shoes of her hunter and she recognised them instantly. Light in colour, foreign looking and expensive, an unusual buckle fastening which had drawn her attention to them earlier. She stiffened in fear. Often in the past she had considered how she would react if confronted by an attacker. She had envisaged quite different circumstances, not this trapped situation. And this man was an American. Everyone knew that Americans carried guns in the way that Englishmen carried wallets; and not only American men. She had once read that even old ladies in that country carried small hand-guns in their handbags. Even *her* niece had been shot!

Slowly and determinedly the beam moved on around the field then returned to linger with hostile concentration on the old oak. Her breath on hold she waited for him to move closer. Relentlessly the spotlight held the tree captive. Despite its girth it did not completely conceal the front wheel and she waited for the flashlight to expose the small portion of wheel-rim that protruded. After an eternity it retreated to seek in the blackness elsewhere.

She released her breath and felt it mist on the frosty air, then cast a brief glance down at the wheel rim. Mercifully time had dulled it with rust and it had not reflected in the probing ray. More anxious moments passed before the slow searching beam retreated.

Unfamiliar with the field terrain James Maddison turned back towards the lane. She heard him mutter something but the words were lost in the crunch of his footsteps.

As he went out through the gate he cursed profanely. He had expected her to be within sight on the other side of the hedge. 'Bitch won't escape me, not after I've been to all this trouble,' he swore again. When he reached the car he sat for a few minutes wondering whether there was a clear way across the field to gain access to the house or if she would be forced to return to the lane. Suspecting that she might find a way through the hedge further along he switched on the car engine and lights and drove the Bentley slowly forward, his eyes searching the road ahead.

*   *   *

The blackness in the lane was total. Sally Lane peered hard but could see no sign of any car light. The lane was fairly narrow and winding and she decided to go to the next curve. Wobbling uncomfortably she pedalled on, the pain in her foot taking second place to her concern.

An owl flew close startling her and she overbalanced on the awkward bicycle. As she remounted she heard the sound of a car and saw headlamps suddenly switched on in the distance. With relief but still puzzled, she turned the old upright around and rode unsteadily back in the direction of the house.

Eyes alert and peering into the darkness James Maddison crouched over the driving wheel. In the distance now he caught sight of the wavering rear-light ahead. The faint illumination from the dials on the dashboard showed a maniacal expression of triumph on his face now as he put his foot down hard on the accelerator and drove full tilt at the small red zig-zagging glow. In the car headlamps he clearly saw the over-long coat hanging darkly at each side of the back wheel of the unmistakable old upright and aimed the Bentley straight at it.

★　★　★

As the sound of the car receded Martha Oakes mobilised her freezing limbs and rubbed life back into her numb fingers. For a moment or two she stood stamping to restore circulation to her feet, while she tried to judge whether it would be safer to return to her sister's cottage, or risk the distance to the house. He might come back to look for her before she reached the village. Even though she knew the lane well enough to ride without the guiding cycle-lamp there were not enough gaps in the hedge through which she could escape at the first warning ray of car headlights. The curve of the lane would give only brief notice. By keeping to the path at the field side of the hedge she should be able to make it to the house; although on foot there was no access across country on account of the thick bushes which bordered various parts of the estate. She would eventually have to cut through a gap in the hedge and travel on the road again before reaching the entrance gates.

Only now did it strike her what mortal danger she had placed herself in. With shock she realised that she would never be safe from this man until the death of Emily Penne and the estate had been shared between them. She couldn't go to the police. They would want to know why she thought he intended to harm her. She was just deciding to chance it back to her sister's cottage when she heard the crash.

★ ★ ★

Aided by desperation the twitching in Emily Penne's fingers became a stronger, more definite movement. With concentrated effort of will she lowered her right hand to contact the wheel of the chair. Then with all the frail strength she could muster in her feet she used them for leverage by pushing against the furniture, starting with the coffee table which was closest. In this manner she succeeded in turning the chair. Using furniture to aid movement she continued slowly backwards across the room towards the door.

Panting from exertion she reached the hall and paused briefly to recover her breath. On the marble floor the wheels of the chair moved more easily, although there was little or no furniture here to aid her. A giant vase that contained a philodendron stood on the floor and she pushed against it, breathing heavily from the effort. The vase rocked and settled back into position again and the chair travelled a few yards backwards. Determination lent her strength as she pushed against a heavy carved wooden bench. This gave the wheels enough momentum across the smooth floor to send the chair the remaining distance to the hall-table and the telephone. With painful slowness her hand now moved towards a pencil placed alongside a notepad for messages. Her fingers refused to close around its slimness. After further persever-ance she managed to grasp the pencil by clamping it in the curve of her palm with her thumb.

Laboriously she began to write in large awkwardly formed letters. When she had completed only four and a half of these she heard the sound of screeching car tyres in the lane, then a crash.

She dropped the pencil and listened, thankful that she was wearing her hearing-aid. A few seconds later the car came to a noisy halt just outside in the driveway.

With the aid of her feet and hands against the table she gained enough leverage to send the chair-wheels moving backwards into a shadowed recess in the hall and out of the view of the front entrance doors, one of which was still partly open.

Panting loudly James Maddison entered the hall with a rush and made straight for the drawing room. His expression showed surprise when he saw that the wheelchair with its occupant and Sally Lane were not there. He concluded that she had taken the old lady off to some other room before being overcome by the pills herself. He did not check the coffee cups before bending over the seemingly lifeless form of Charlie. With exerted effort he lifted him fireman fashion onto his shoulder. Although well built himself he staggered under the weight as he carried him out to the car. Concerned only with his present mission he was unaware that he was being observed.

With difficulty he lowered Charlie into the driving seat of the Bentley. Then he straightened up to briefly nurse his strained back before taking a small bottle of whisky from his top-coat pocket. He then attempted to force some of the spirits between Charlie's uncooperative lips. The liquid over-spilled down Charlie's chin and clothes. After making further attempts unsuccessfully he proceeded to pour the spirits over Charlie's clothes. Then he dropped the now empty bottle down beside the car seat. During these last moments of concentration he heard the sound of the telephone ringing. He deduced vaguely that the caller must be the girl Lydie who had gone out for the evening. That had been greatly to his advantage, although he had been concerned that she might arrive back at the house before his plan was completed. It had all been a race against time. Well, he had finished now, she could come and welcome, he'd be gone before she arrived.

★ ★ ★

Breathing heavily from her efforts Emily Penne pushed her shoulder against the wall and strained to move the chair out of the recess and back to the telephone. It rang before she had quite reached it. The sudden unexpected sound startled her for the moment. Her left hand was now close to the

252

loop of the cord and she slipped one arm through this, then brought it back towards the chair with the cord lodged between her wrist and the armrest. Once again she pushed her feet against the table sending the chair-wheels in a backward motion. The cord pulled sideways but the receiver stayed firmly in its cradle and the whole telephone moved towards the edge of the table top. The chair was now resting against the wall once more. Again she pushed her shoulder against this to send the wheels forward and bring the chair back to the telephone table. The cord was now at another angle. She tugged and the receiver was jerked front-ways from its cradle. It fell with a clatter onto the table-top close to the edge, resting on its side. Releasing her hand from the cord she moved her fingers across to a small silver bell close by and tried to grasp it in her fingers. It slipped from her hold and toppled over, rolling from its own momentum with a prolonged metallic sound on the polished wood until it finally settled and was still. She lowered her face to the mouthpiece of the receiver as far as she was able and as loudly as was in the limits of her power she attempted to speak. The resultant mumbling sounds brought tears of frustration to her eyes and dripped onto the table top.

After a renewed attempt to phone the house Lydie was about to replace the receiver when she heard the clatter and tinkling of the bell as it rolled to a standstill on the table-top. 'Hello what's happening? Who's there?' She heard the urgent mumblings on the other end of the line and called across the hall at Tanglewood, 'Clive — there must be something wrong at the house! Emily's on the line. I can't imagine what's happened. I heard that little bell that's kept beside the phone on the downstairs hall-table. We'd best leave immediately.'

'Don't hang up.' Instantly he was beside her and she handed him the receiver.

He listened briefly to the insistent mumblings then said, 'It's Clive here Emily. If you're alone will you try to ring the bell again.' He heard the faint metallic sound of the bell rolling as Emily Penne reached out clumsily to touch it. 'I'm going to hang up now Emily and I shall come straight over.' He replaced the receiver. 'Surely they can't have gone out and left her alone!'

Lydie shook her head emphatically as they went to fetch their outdoor coats. 'Charlie would never do that. Something must have happened!'

With a sob of relief Emily Penne raised her head from the phone and straightened up in the chair which she started to propel towards the front door.

★   ★   ★

James Maddison took one last satisfied look at the drugged figure of Charlie slumped over the driving wheel and pulled aside his glove to check the time. He let out an oath as he saw that his watch was missing. He made a hasty and frantic search in the dark beside the driving seat but his hand did not contact anything other than the empty whisky bottle. He switched on his flashlight to search more thoroughly. 'It must be here somewhere,' he muttered, panicking now in his haste to be away. The gold band must have got caught up in Charlie's clothes and been dragged off. He would just have to shift the dead weight again. After a few more moments of frantic and unfruitful searching he straightened up again. With the torch he made a hasty search along the path that he'd taken to get to the car. But he found no watch. 'Must have fallen off in the house,' he muttered and turned towards the front door. He made a sound of surprise as he saw the wheelchair framed against the hall-light in the doorway and the dark silhouette of the old lady watching him.

On top of his panic to be gone the sight unnerved him as he perceived that she was not as incapacitated as he'd thought her to be. Also she obviously hadn't drunk her coffee. Which meant that she'd seen him drop the pills into the cups.

Oh what the hell — she was no threat. Unless . . . ? He began to have doubts. Just how much power had she in her hands? After all she'd got the bloody chair to the doorway. What if she managed to write! How much had she seen? Too bloody much, that seemed sure now! He strode over to the entrance and pushed the wheelchair aside roughly as he entered the house. In the drawing room he made a hasty search of the floor and found his watch close to the wingchair where Charlie had been sitting. 'F . . . ing watch,' he muttered, relieved that he'd noticed it missing before he'd left the scene altogether. This wasn't the first time it had been caught up and become unfastened. Should be more secure, goddamn cost enough! He placed the watch in his pocket and returned to the hall. On his way to the front door he glanced across at the table and saw that the phone was off the hook. He stopped abruptly, attention now on Emily Penne still at the spot where he had shoved the wheelchair aside.

With angry movements he strode across and grasped the back of the chair. Viciously he thrust it forward to the front porch and down the steps. The old lady held on tightly as she was jarred spitefully with each drop of the wheels.

Facing the chair towards the back of the house he ran with it along the side path, then sent it careering violently forward into the darkness beyond into the unseen area unlit by any house lights. As he watched it disappear from view he muttered — 'There, see if you can survive that you old hag.' Might have his share of the inheritance sooner than expected. She wouldn't last long in this freezing temperature and she wasn't wearing any top-coat.

With his customary confidence he figured that he would never be connected with the crime he'd committed in Berry Lane. Silence was assured from Sally Lane under the threat of exposure as his accomplice. In too deep herself she wouldn't dare risk her neck, even for the Baines guy. Drugging *her* coffee as well had been a wise move. What she didn't know she couldn't tell. No one but her and the old lady knew that he'd been in the house: Apart from the Baines guy and he didn't count; who would believe his story! And Martha Oakes was off his list of obstructors now.

As he drove off in the hired car its headlamps picked out the dark crumpled shape on the grass verge in the lane. One of the wheels of the old upright was uppermost. He slowed only briefly as he passed. Then the car picked up speed and he headed for his London hotel.

The distant glow of light warned Martha Oakes of the approaching car and she ducked down behind the hedge. For a while after hearing the sound of the crash she had remained where she was, ears alert. She had heard the car drive on in the direction of the house. Cautiously she had moved away from her hiding place behind the tree and onto the path bordering the field on the inside of the hedge. Several times she had paused to listen for sounds of the car returning, and had wondered if the American had parked it again and was waiting in the lane. As a car passed now she attempted to see its colour through the foliage of the hedge, but it was moving too fast to distinguish in the headlights. But she knew that it must be the American; rarely did traffic pass through the lane at night. Alarmed and curious about the crash she chanced a bolder approach now. She continued on to where she knew there was a narrow gap in the hedge where she could squeeze through with the bicycle and return

258

to the road. Thankful that she hadn't chanced returning to the village she waited in the lane for the sound of the car to die away. Then with the cycle lamp switched on again she rode fast towards the house.

Clive Wessley brought the car sharply to a halt at the unexpected sight of the Bentley parked in the middle of the driveway with its headlamps on and its door open. 'What the Devil . . . '

'What on earth has happened here!' Alarmed Lydie got from the car and ran to investigate. Clive was close on her heels.

They found Charlie slumped over the wheel just as James Maddison had left him.

'My God! What . . . ' Lydie wrinkled her nose as the smell of the spirits wafted from the car. She stepped aside while Clive leaned in and took Charlie by the shoulders to ease him upright in the seat. He made a grimace, 'Whisky.'

'But Charlie never touches spirits Clive. You know that. I don't understand.'

Instantly Clive took command. 'Go on inside and make some strong black coffee. And check that Emily's all right. I'll bring Charlie in.'

This took a little time. With difficulty he eased Charlie's dead weight out of the seat and onto his shoulder then carried him into the house. As he entered the hall Lydie was running down the stairs.

'I can't find Emily! Or her niece. They're not in the drawing room or in their bedrooms!'

Clive carried Charlie into the kitchen and lowered him onto a chair.

'Soak a cloth in cold water. We'll have to revive him so he can explain what the Devil's been happening here.'

Quickly Lydie obeyed and held the icy towel to Charlie's face. 'Wake up Charlie!' She stopped briefly to shake him by his shoulders. 'Where's Emily Charlie?'

The kettle boiled and she went to the stove to make the coffee.

Clive Wessley took over the cold wet towel and held it to Charlie's face, at intervals removing it to slap at the unconscious face. Then he put the cloth aside. 'They *must* be about somewhere. I don't understand this at all! I'll check the other rooms down here and upstairs.' He left the kitchen and sprinted up the stairs. After making a quick search in all the rooms and bathrooms upstairs and down he returned to the hall to inspect the telephone which still lay on the table where it had fallen. Non-plussed he went back to the kitchen. 'There's no one in the house at al!'

'Martha can't be home from the cinema

yet.' Lydie was now trying to force cold water from a glass into Charlie's uncooperative mouth. 'The coffee's too hot yet.'

'I'm going outside to look around. Where can I find a torch?' Clive was already opening drawers and cupboards as he spoke.

'Top left drawer.' Lydie pointed.

He grasped one of two torches from the drawer and as he hurried out called over his shoulder, 'Cool the coffee with cold water.'

'Of course! Why didn't I think of that.' Lydie took the steaming cup to the tap and topped it with water. Before making an attempt to force the liquid between Charlie's lips she tested that it was now cool enough. She grimaced, she couldn't abide black coffee and knew that Charlie couldn't either, which might evoke a quicker response. After several more attempts she succeeded with difficulty in forcing his lips apart and some of the coffee into his reluctant mouth.

'Come on Charlie wake up,' she begged. 'Please wake up and tell us what's been going on here.' She held the wet cloth beneath his chin to catch the spill from the cup. After a moment, to her great relief, he coughed. This had the effect of rousing him slightly. She forced him to swallow more of the strong dark brew.

He choked and coughed again but she

persisted. 'You must drink it Charlie.' When she'd managed to get him to swallow half of the coffee, except that which had been spilt in the process, she put aside the cup. Again she shook him by his shoulders, her voice raised in desperation as he sank back against the chair. 'Charlie you must wake up. *Please!*' She applied the cold wet cloth to his face again. After a few more anxious moments had passed he stirred and his eyes flickered open briefly before closing again. 'Charlie wake up,' she shook his shoulders again. 'What's been happening here?'

He stirred again, his hands went to his head and he moved it from side to side. Gradually he fought to revive himself and keep his eyes open. Suddenly he brought his hands away from his head and wiped them across his mouth as he made a grimace of disgust at the smell of spirits. Desperately he tried to shake off the heavy sleep that was weighing him down. Bemused he tried to focus his eyes while he struggled to surface from the somnolent effects of the pills. 'What? What . . . ?' Still under the influence of sleep his words were indistinct.

'Drink this,' Lydie urged putting the coffee to his lips once more and holding it there until he'd almost finished what was left. She put aside the cup and ordered. 'Stand up

Charlie. You must walk about. Come on. Lean on me.' He seemed incapable of movement. She slapped at his face, then tugged at him in attempt to pull him up from the chair.

He ran his hands through his hair and shook his head to throw off drowsiness as he attempted to get up. Twice he fell back onto the chair. At the third attempt he stood swaying unsteadily. She put her shoulder beneath his arm and braced herself against his weight. 'Try to walk Charlie,' she coaxed as he moved his unsteady legs forward.

Lydie guided him out into the hall. 'Try to think Charlie it's very important. Something has happened here this evening. Where is everyone?'

Charlie blinked several times in an effort to concentrate on what she was saying. 'Everyone. What — what? I don't know . . . ' his words petered out and he swayed against her. 'Water. I must have . . . '

She led him back to the kitchen and still supporting him filled a glass with cold water and handed it to him, ready to grasp it if it fell from his hand.

He drank it down fast after which she ordered him to douse his face under the cold running tap. In his docile state he obeyed.

She handed him a cloth to dry his face and hair. 'Now Charlie tell me what happened here. Where is everyone?'

After shining the torch in every direction at the front of the house Clive Wessley closed the door of the Bentley and went back into the house. Immediately he returned to the kitchen to help Lydie. Together they supported Charlie, guiding him into the hall where there was more free space for the three of them to move around. In an attempt to penetrate the soporific state of Charlie's drugged senses he spoke in a demanding tone. 'Now think man where is Emily and her niece. I can't find them in the house. And we had a strange telephone call. Did you drive them somewhere?'

The words, on top of the cold water dousing, had some effect on Charlie. He stared, not comprehending. Still dazed he glanced about. 'Not in the house!' His own voice revived him further and he perked up. 'But they, they were in the . . . ' he turned to point in the direction of the drawing room. 'We were all in there.' Unaided now he walked unsteadily towards the drawing room. 'The American chap left and . . . ' As he spoke he entered the room and glanced about him. Alert now he continued. 'Where's Emily. She was in the wheelchair by the fire and

264

— and — ' he pointed to the wing-back. 'I was sitting there. He made coffee and brought it over to me and . . . I must have fallen a . . .'

Before he could finish Lydie cut in. 'We found you out in the Bentley Charlie with whisky spilt over you and an empty bottle by the seat. How did you get out there? Think — think Charlie.'

Looking bemused now he shook his head slowly. 'I don't know. I only remember that I drank the coffee that he brought over to me. I can't remember anything more after that. I must have fallen asleep almost instantly I drank it.' As if Lydie's words had just sunk in he continued, 'Did you say car? I was in the car! But that's not possible. I always put it in the garage after use. No . . . wait — I remember — the tree. I brought the tree back in the car . . . and I parked the car in the driveway to unload it. That's right, I meant to put it away later but I found the American was already here. And he stayed late.' He rubbed his hands across his eyes and through his hair. 'How did Emily get up to her room? I always carry her up, but I know I didn't.'

Clive Wessley interrupted him. 'She didn't. We can't find her. I've looked all over the house, there's no one here at all, not even

Martha. You say that the American chap was here?'

'Yes he was here to dinner. He stayed late. He handed round coffee . . . I drank mine. I think he left about that time. I don't remember anything after that. I know his being here appeared to bother Emily. I don't think she liked him. She seemed quite disturbed all evening. He came in a hired car.' Concern was fast reviving Charlie.

'I'm going to take another look around outside.' Clive Wessley picked up the torch as he spoke. 'Lydie get a torch for Charlie. You must both come out and help me search.'

★   ★   ★

The glow of the small red rear-light above the twisted wheel of the old upright caught the eye of Martha Oakes as she came upon the scene. Cautiously she dismounted and approached, then gasped in shock as she saw the results of the crash she'd heard. Then, in the lamplight of the bicycle she was riding, she saw the black shape lying motionless alongside. Instantly her mind grasped the situation. Although completely baffled as to why the victim was wearing the old black coat and on the flat-tyred bike from the garage, she was in no doubt at all by whose hand she came to be lying in the lane injured. Common sense told her that it was a clear case of mistaken identity. She bent over for closer inspection. The girl looked dead. Hard to tell in the darkness. She felt a wrist, there seemed to be no pulse. She straightened up and remounted the bicycle, then pedalled hard towards the house. When she turned the curve in the long drive she saw the two cars and Clive Wessley with the torch. He came towards her before she had even dismounted. 'Ah Martha there you are. Thank heaven you're back. Perhaps you can . . . '

She cut his words short. 'In the lane . . . hurry . . . the girl — an accident. I think she may be dead!' She remounted the bicycle. 'I'll show you where . . . '

He got into his car, turned it about face and followed. Moments later he was bending over the small dark-coated figure on the verge. After feeling for a pulse he said, 'Get back to the house Martha and call an ambulance. For God's sake hurry! I think she's still alive.' He removed his top-coat and covered the motionless form.

★ ★ ★

When James Maddison had callously launched the wheelchair into motion along the dark path it had veered and struck a glancing blow to one of the rocks which bordered a flower bed at the corner of the house. Nudged off-course it had changed direction, its wheels gathering momentum as they rolled down a gently sloping bank. With impact it had come to rest against dense shrubs. The spot was in total darkness at the side of the house where no windows were at present lit.

Charlie now fully recovered from the effects of the drugged coffee had joined up with Lydie in the search. Martha Oakes, back from the scene in the lane and still shocked at her narrow escape, had also been dispatched to help.

Clive Wessley had followed the ambulance in his car to Nightingale Hospital. He intended to stay at the bedside of the victim hoping she would regain consciousness and give some account of how she came to be lying injured beside the old upright in Berry Lane, and dressed in Martha Oakes's coat.

At this moment Martha Oakes, by the light of her own torch, was following the path that would lead to the wheelchair. She was as puzzled as the others about the disappearance of Emily Penne. She was wondering if the American had murdered her too and dumped her somewhere on the estate, perhaps further away from the house. She was even more curious as to how this could have been carried out without the knowledge of Charlie. Anyway she had no intentions of going far afield in this freezing temperature to search. She didn't expect to find the wheelchair. At this point her torch-ray lit up a dark corner ahead. She was about to turn around to go back inside when a faint sound caught her attention and she paused briefly. 'Cats,' she muttered and moved on.

The sound reached her ears again and she half turned in its direction. It didn't sound quite so cat-like now. She retraced her steps towards the dark corner where the sound became more distinct. Warily now she moved forward, sending the beam of light before her. First it picked out a shiny wheel-rim, then gradually climbed until it highlighted the frozen features and startled eyes of the old lady.

Martha Oakes stared, dumbfounded at the unexpected sight in the spotlight. Slowly she went closer, down the grassy slope, until she was barely two feet from the wheelchair. About to reach out to grasp the back of this she changed her mind and her hand fell away. Without a word she turned and strode off back to the house. Feeling no compassion her mind now tried to speculate on why Sally Lane had been in the lane dressed in the old black coat, and Emily Penne outside in the garden abandoned to the frosty night. Of one thing only she was certain at present; if Sally Lane died, she herself would still be in mortal danger from the American whom she could identify as the murderer. But if the girl survived, and the will read, the way ahead might be safe. The old lady couldn't possibly survive the night in this freezing temperature, especially in her present fragile state.

Just as she reached the front entrance Charlie appeared from the opposite direction, having made an extensive search at that side of the property. 'Nothing that way,' she assured him, indicating the path from which she had come.

Ignoring her Charlie continued on along the path she had just left. He and Lydie together had covered every part of the garden except at this side of the house. Then she had run back inside to switch on the lights in the downstairs rooms to highlight this more secluded aspect of the garden. Having now done this she hurried back out to catch up with him. Seconds later the beam of Charlie's flashlight ended their search.

★ ★ ★

'It's a miracle she survived. The hedge must have sheltered her. It's as well you were on hand though Miss Collins.' Doctor Macalistair rested a hand briefly on Lydie's shoulder as he spoke. 'It's a good thing you found her when you did. She'd not have survived long out there in that temperature. Let's hope the police throw some light on the matter soon. What's the latest news on the poor young lassie?'

'Critical I'm afraid Doctor. I telephoned ten minutes ago for news. Clive is still at the hospital waiting in the hope that she regains consciousness.'

Except for the brief phone calls to the hospital and the doctor, Lydie had not left the side of Emily Penne since they had found her and brought her back into the house. Charlie had carried her upstairs to settle her in her bed after instructing Martha to make hot drinks.

The doctor shook his head slowly as if finding it hard to credit the mysterious and traumatic events of the evening. 'Emily could not have got out there by herself. She could never have managed the front steps. I'll go on downstairs and wait until Clive gets back.'

Downstairs Charlie poured some brandy for the doctor and handed it to him as he came into the drawing room. 'You need something to warm you. Sorry we had to call you out on such a cold night.'

'Thanks Charlie.' Doctor Macalistair readily accepted the glass and seated himself before the fire which Charlie had just banked up. He had been given a brief outline of what had occurred in-as-much as they knew of the facts themselves. Charlie had related what little he could.

They had already questioned Martha Oakes but gained very little information. To protect her own backside she had decided to keep her lips clamped and say as little as possible. She had simply told them that the American was a dinner guest just for the evening; and about the borrowed coat and bicycle. She'd had no choice without drawing attention to herself. Even she had no clue as to why the girl had been in the lane and wearing the black coat.

Since then she had kept to the kitchen. She felt no remorse for her callousness in deliberately leaving Emily Penne out in the garden to perish from the cold; and at the same time was relieved that she was incapable of telling tales. Fear of the American was uppermost in her mind at present. When they caught him there was a good chance that he would implicate her. Of course she would deny anything he said. No one could prove that she'd had any previous contact with him; unless the girl recovered and confessed everything. But by the look of things there seemed little hope of her survival. She was deeply curious herself to know what had taken place in the house after she'd left to go to the cinema.

A few minutes ago she had been stopped by Charlie from emptying the two cups of cold coffee that had been left untouched. He had also instructed her not to wash the cup used by himself.

Charlie had changed from his drink-soiled clothes into clean ones. Those discarded he intended to keep as evidence. Angry, he itched to get his hands on the American.

Lydie entered the drawing room. 'I need more hot water bottles Charlie. Will you ask Martha to bring some up. I don't want to leave Emily on her own or I'd do it myself.'

Charlie went instantly into the kitchen to pass on the request to the housekeeper since only she knew where the bottles were kept. As Lydie was returning upstairs the telephone rang. Charlie dashed into the hall to answer.

'Clive here Charlie. Have you found — '

'Yes,' Charlie cut in and explained what had happened. Then asked, 'Any news?'

'Still not regained consciousness and in intensive care. Charlie I've arranged for you to be driven to headquarters to make what statement you can about the affair. They'll arrange for you to be examined to determine that the coffee was drugged. They'll want to analyse what was left in the cup and the full cups that weren't touched. Also they'll verify that you had not been drinking and that the spirits were planted on your clothes. All for your own protection of course. Just make certain that Martha doesn't empty those cups.'

'Yes I've already told her. I'll make sure they're not touched.'

It was both fortunate and unfortunate that Sally Lane had left her coffee. Unfortunate in that she would not be where she was now had she drank it. Fortunate because it was evidence in Charlie's favour.

The doctor stayed quite late. At intervals he went upstairs to check on the old lady's condition and to sit awhile at the bedside. At present she was dozing. Her ordeal in the garden and attempts to attract attention had left her in a state of exhaustion. 'Just come down a wee while and warm yourself by the fire Miss Collins,' the doctor coaxed. 'Emily will be all right on her own now that she's sleeping.'

Lydie nodded and accompanied him downstairs to the drawing room. Charlie related the telephone message from Clive Wessley.

'Emily mustn't be told about the accident yet,' advised the doctor as he prepared to leave the house. 'If you have any concerns during the night call me immediately. I shall look in first thing tomorrow morning otherwise. Let's hope we have some better news of the lassie by then.'

As he passed through the hall he paused to eye the Christmas tree. 'Well it's certainly not turning out to be the Christmas you had all planned.'

'No indeed,' Charlie agreed. 'I got the tree to make Christmas a bit brighter for Emily.'

They accompanied him to the door and wished him goodnight.

Lydie closed the door after him. 'It's quite obvious to me that the American is responsible for everything. But why? What possible reason? Jealousy perhaps? Maybe he was more than just her employer. A crime of passion as they say. He must have deliberately planned the whole thing in advance so that you'd be blamed.'

Bemused Charlie shook his head. 'Doesn't make any sense Lyd. She was in the drawing room with me when he left. I can't imagine why she left the house at all! Especially on that old bike! In any case he must have come

275

back into the house. Or how the hell did I get planted in the car!' Charlie clenched his fist and looked uncharacteristically angry. 'My God if I ever get my hands on the bastard!'

Lydie patted his arm to calm him. 'The police will deal with him. They'll be here soon.' They returned into the warmth of the drawing room. 'I wish we knew something more definite about the American though. I never even saw him. Let's try Martha.'

'No.' Charlie lowered his voice, 'I don't trust her Lyd. She came from the direction where we found Emily. I actually passed her. Yet she told me that she'd already searched that area.'

'But it was probably before I put the lights on in the room that overlooks that spot.'

'Well my torch showed the chair clearly enough. It's no use Lyd I don't like the woman. There's something underhanded about her.'

'Well she's the only one who can tell us about the American. After all he was a dinner guest. I wish now that I'd hung on long enough to meet him when he arrived, but Clive's mother was especially serving an early dinner. She and his father were going out visiting.'

In the kitchen Martha Oakes was pouring boiling water into a teapot. She did not turn as Lydie entered and spoke. 'Have you remembered the name of the dinner guest Miss Oakes?'

The reply was brusque and disinterested. 'I have not. If it was given I paid no attention.' She had no intentions of offering any information that could lead the trail to herself, not while Sally Lane was alive. Of course — if the girl died — well that was another matter altogether. Then for her own safety she would tell the police about the American soon enough. Without the girl there would be no hope of any share in the legacy; and he would not be likely to leave the only witness to his crime alive to tell any tales.

'Charlie is sure that no surname was mentioned to him. I expect Clive will go through Emily's correspondence from her niece in case she may have mentioned him in her letters,' Lydie persisted to the hostile back. She felt sure that Martha Oakes knew more than she was telling. When no further response came she returned to the bedside of Emily Penne who was still dozing; the tot of brandy that she'd been given having done its work.

★　★　★

In his hotel James Maddison poured himself a large whisky. This he took with him as he left the room and went across the corridor to knock on the door of the room opposite his. Without waiting for a reply he turned the knob and entered. 'Hello there,' he called as he closed the door behind him. 'You said look in for a drink sometime. Hope I'm not too late for you.' His manner was cool and confident despite his recent devious activities.

The television was switched on and there was a half-empty gin bottle on the coffee table beside a settee, over the back of which a female head bobbed into view. 'Oh hello there. Come right in. I haven't the foggiest what the time is but whatever — it's not too late. I've spent the evening alone watching some dreadful American film. All violence, screeching tyres and car crashes! It's no wonder that your country is riddled with crime. And your actors! Surely the world's worst.'

James Maddison didn't give a bloody toss what she thought of American actors, although pressed for an opinion he would have agreed with her.

He strode over to the television and switched it off. 'In that case we don't have to watch the crappy stuff do we.' He seated himself beside her. She was twirling an empty glass between her fingers with a bored expression on her face and sounded tipsy.

'Cheers,' he said and drained his glass. 'Let me pour you another.' He took the glass from her and refilled it from the gin bottle.

'There's whisky on the sideboard,' she offered.

He rose and filled the glass he had brought in with him.

'So you've been on your lonesome all evening then.'

'I have.'

'Well what d'ya know — so have I. We can spend the rest of it together.'

'What time is it then? It could be two in the morning for all I know.'

He made a display of consulting his watch, then held his wrist in front of her eyes. Obligingly she studied the watch-face and said, 'Half past ten! Is that all. I thought it was much . . . oh well never mind,' she took another swig from her glass.

He held his wrist close to her ear now. 'Is it ticking okay?'

She listened briefly. 'Yes it's ticking.'

'Then ten-thirty it is.' He was satisfied that his cunning move in winding the watch back had worked and her drink befuddled mind did not question the two hour time loss. She could be his perfect alibi if it became necessary.

When he'd left the hotel earlier in the afternoon to go to Grandstone House he had not checked out at the reception desk; instead he had deliberately left his room unlocked so that he need not check in again for the key on his return.

The story which the Baines guy would tell was going to look pretty feeble when he told the police that a perfect stranger had planted him in the Bentley. Sally Lane could not corroborate his story without incriminating herself. Now that the bitch of a housekeeper was out of the way and the old lady practically expired, the estate was as good as theirs; the money almost within his grasp now.

Well satisfied with the way he had dealt with things he slipped his arm across the shoulders of the girl as she swallowed more gin. Not one to delay pressing home his advantage, at work or play, he put his lips close to her ear and whispered, 'Yes it's only ten-thirty. We've got all night.'

18

CHRISTMAS EVE

As James Maddison surfaced from sleep he put his hand to his throbbing head. Abruptly he sat up in the bed and glanced about him. Recollection returned and he discovered that he was still in the girl's bed. He called her name. When there was no reply he recalled that she'd mentioned something about an early hairdressing appointment and a modelling assignment — or was it an interview for one? He saw that she'd left a note on the dressing table. He got out of the bed and read the message on the slip of paper. It merely said — 'Leave my key at the reception desk.'

He glanced at his watch still on his wrist and saw that it was only eight o'clock. Then he recalled that he'd wound the hands back two hours for the benefit of an alibi. He went into the bathroom and splashed cold water on his face before dressing and returning to his own room where he immediately rang for coffee and aspirin.

Fifteen minutes later he picked up the telephone and dialled. After a brief interval he heard a voice at the other end stating, 'Grandstone House. Martha Oakes speaking.'

In shock his jaw sagged, his face turned grey and he almost dropped the receiver. As he slowly replaced this he heard the voice repeat the words.

Hands shaking he drank the rest of his coffee then went to pour himself some whisky, with soda this time. 'What the hell!' He muttered. 'Have I gone crazy!' Having just heard the voice of the woman he thought he had run down and left for dead he wondered if his mind was playing tricks on account of his heavy drinking the previous night.

After seating himself to steady his legs he rang for more coffee. Fifteen minutes later he dialled the Grandstone House number again. This time a different voice answered. 'Grandstone House. Lydie Collins speaking.'

Prepared this time he placed a handkerchief across his mouth and attempted to speak with an English accent. 'May I speak with Miss Carpenter please.'

There were a few moments delay at the other end before a reply came. 'I'm afraid there's been an accident. Miss Carpenter was knocked down by a car and seriously injured last night. She's in hospital. May I ask who's — ?'

As he lowered the receiver without making

a reply the voice was still speaking. Shaken he stared down at it as realisation of what must have occurred sank into his still befuddled mind.

He had been sure that it was the Oakes woman . . . her old fashioned bicycle . . . the long black coat. Recapping on the time he was in the lane last evening he paced the room. How had the Oakes bitch eluded him? How! And what the bloody hell was Sally Lane doing out there wearing that old fashioned coat! She'd been in the drawing room about to drink her coffee, just as he'd planned, when he'd left the house.

He glanced at his watch then darted across to switch on the radio and was in time to hear the Big Ben chimes by which he promptly put his watch right. Every muscle tense he listened for the news. Soon it came, words that registered in snatches. 'Hit and run accident . . . critical . . . ' Did that mean she was not expected to live? Sometimes people made miraculous recoveries. Without her there was no inheritance — no money. He switched the radio off as the reader moved on to other news. He had not registered into the hotel under his own name. He'd covered his tracks for the previous evening. The girl could vouch for him if it became necessary. The guy Baines was in a very shaky position on his own . . .

But now the Oakes woman could back up his story knowing that it was herself who had been the intended target in the lane. He paced again and muttered while he plotted his next move. 'I'll deal with the Oakes bitch yet; then I'll get the hell out of here.'

★ ★ ★

Clive Wessley stretched his long legs and shifted his weight on the hard chair at the bedside in Nightingale Hospital. His eyes had barely left the ashen face surrounded by bandages. Doctors and nurses had been constantly in and out of the room. Now for a few brief moments he was alone with the patient in intensive care. Alone with his thoughts and musings on a merry-go-round of seeking a motive. In his past experience this was invariably any one of four; possibly a combination of all: Gain, hate, jealousy or insanity; the last one hardly a motive, merely a condition. Things looked bad for Charlie, although the drugged coffee was in his favour. There was the question of the spirits on his clothes. Lydie had insisted that Charlie never touched strong drink, and he himself had never seen him do so. He believed

Charlie. Although he mightn't be all that Emily thought him to be, and she judged as she found and not on hearsay, he couldn't be too bad or he wouldn't have been Lydie's closest friend for so many years.

The American was highly suspect. Calls had to be put out in attempt to trace him. But with little to identify him at present there seemed scarce hope of that until he made a move to leave the country. Sooner or later he would be detained at the airport. At least Charlie would be able to identify him, as would Martha Oakes. And that was another puzzling aspect. Despite the gravity of the situation she had little to say of help even though she had served dinner to the chap and must have been introduced to him.

The door of the ward opened to admit the nursing sister and he heard the distant sound of carol singing from somewhere in the interior of the hospital. The sound was immediately cut off with the closing of the door. 'Still no sign?' she asked.

He shook his head.

She came to the bedside and stood looking down at the wan face for a few moments. 'You must be tired Inspector. Not a very pleasant Christmas for you.'

'Nor for a good many, particularly this young woman.'

She nodded and sighed as she turned to leave. When she'd gone he took from his pocket the small writing pad which he'd found beside the telephone on the hall table in Grandstone House. He was glad that he'd had the presence of mind to pick it up when he'd replaced the receiver. It gave him some small clue to work on during his immobile wait. He studied again the large spidery scrawl of the unfinished word, A MERI. At first glance he had taken it to be an attempt by Emily to write A MERRY CHRISTMAS; perhaps an exercise to try to regain the use of her fingers and at the same time a message to communicate with those about her. Now after much thought and study of the letters he deduced that it might well be the interrupted efforts to write the word AMERICAN. She had obviously been at the hall table earlier when they'd heard the bell and her mumbling attempts to speak.

The door of the ward opened and again he heard the carol singers. 'Silent night . . . ' Silent indeed for the girl in the bed he mused.

'I thought you might like some tea Inspector Wessley.' The nursing sister placed a tray containing sandwiches and tea on the bedside cupboard.

'Thank you Sister.'

She checked her patient and as she turned to leave he asked, 'Do you think there might be such a thing as a set of alphabet letters in the nursery or playroom? If so I should like to borrow them if I may. I would need to take them away with me and wouldn't keep them any longer than necessary. I've had an idea. I believe they could help me with my investigations about the accident.' He nodded towards the silent figure in the bed.

'Why yes I'm sure there must be. I'll go and look myself.'

Half an hour later, having posted another Scotland Yard detective at the bedside Clive Wessley left the hospital with a parcel under his arm and an idea in his mind. Minutes later he headed his car back towards Redcliffe and Grandstone House, eager to put his idea to the test.

When he arrived Martha Oakes answered his knock. As he stepped hurriedly into the hall he asked, 'Is Lydie upstairs with Emily?'

'Yes. How is the girl? Has she regained consc — ?'

He cut in, 'Not yet.' As he went towards the stairs he thought — That's the most Martha Oakes has ever said to me in one verbal contact; usually only get one word replies — two at most.

On entering the bedroom he saw that

Lydie had fallen asleep on the little chaise longue. No doubt exhausted after long hours of anxiety and lack of sleep for she'd not yet gone to her bed. For a few moments he stood gazing down at her pale face. From the hospital he had telephoned her earlier. He had found her close to tears as she told him that Charlie had been taken along to police headquarters to give an account of the last few hours. She had known this had to be of course as he was the only one at present who could throw any light at all on what had happened. 'Charlie would never hurt anyone believe me,' she had said. She was certainly very fond of her childhood friend. Loyal too. But even without her verbal character reference he knew that Charlie was not their man. Yet there was a great mystery to clear up, and until the injured girl regained consciousness enough to talk they were all going to be left guessing. Unless his idea worked.

He turned now to glance at the bed. Emily looked as if she was sleeping. He seated himself on the small vacant space on the chaise next to Lydie and touched her face lightly. As she stirred he spoke her name softly. He would have preferred not to disturb her sleep but his business was urgent.

She opened her eyes and saw him.

Immediately she became wide awake. He kissed her briefly. 'Hello darling. Sorry I had to wake you.'

'Oh Clive thank heaven you're back. I must have dozed off. How is — ?'

'No change yet. Still unconscious, but there's hope. Listen. I've had an idea. I want to try it out immediately and you'll have to help me.' As he was speaking he unwrapped the parcel.

Lydie went across to the bed. 'By the way Clive there have been two phone calls and I don't know who from. Martha answered the first but the caller rang off without speaking. I answered the second. It was a man and he asked for Miss Carpenter. When I told him about the accident and that she was in hospital he rang off without another word. Didn't even ask which hospital.'

'Strange! Sounds suspicious.' Clive Wessley took the alphabet set across to the bed. 'Look at this. Magnetic letters. Should suit perfectly. Now tell me about that last call — exactly what he said and how he sounded. Was it the American?'

'Well I think he did have an American accent in disguise. His voice sounded muffled — as though he was trying to disguise it.' Lydie repeated what little the caller had said. Then added, 'He rang off before I could question him or even ask his name.'

As if sensing Clive's presence Emily Penne opened her eyes.

Lydie picked up the hearing-aid from the bedside table where she had put it when Emily had fallen asleep. She placed it in position then seated herself on a chair beside the bed.

Emily Penne's eyes moved to the alphabet letters now on the board which Clive had placed on the bed.

'It would be easier if you can sit up.' He turned to Lydie. 'Can we . . . '

'Yes of course, so long as she keeps well covered up and warm.' Lydie helped him to ease the old lady to a sitting position in the bed.

'I have an idea Emily which could help us all if you feel up to it.' Clive spoke in slower than usual speech, uncertain at present just how much she could comprehend since her recent stroke.

Emily Penne nodded again but he saw the fear and concern still in her eyes. He indicated the alphabet board. 'Now I think it may be possible for you to tell us what happened here last evening — or at least give us something to go on. It will take patience and time. These letters are magnetic and will stay on the board wherever they are placed.

He arranged the letters into four groups in alphabetical order. This done he continued, 'Firstly what can you tell us about the American visitor?' To his relief she nodded her head jerkily, indicating that she understood, and he saw the relief in her eyes. 'I want you to think carefully first about what you want to tell us on the board. Then I shall point to each group of letters in turn. If the letter is in that group I want you to nod your head and we'll go on from there. We don't need to bother about spelling. Just a rough attempt will do because duplicate letters are limited. The fact that there are capital ones and small ones at least gives us two of each, so use either. Lydie will write down each letter until we get the word you want. Do you feel up to it?'

She nodded, almost violently, to show her eagerness. Tears of relieved frustration in her eyes, she tried to mumble her agreement at the idea which would provide a way for her to communicate what she so desperately wanted them to know.

Lydie went across to the bureau and moments later settled herself beside the bed with a writing-pad and pen poised ready.

Clive seated himself on the bed with the board and letters facing Emily. 'When you

291

come to the end of all you can tell us just shake your head.'

The idea was successful and the task much quicker than he had anticipated. It showed that Emily Penne's mind was as sharp as ever it had been and that her faculties had not been impaired by either the stroke or her ordeal.

Lydie now read back the words that she'd transcribed onto the pad.

American put something in coffee. Only Charlie drank. He went to sleep instantly. American carried Charlie outside. I followed to hall he pushed me out into garden. Martha saw me but left me.

As the startling revelations came to light on the board Lydie looked shocked. Clive Wessley showed no outward sign of his thoughts except for the raising of his eyebrows. In truth, despite a career in which little surprised him nowadays, he was shaken at what had taken place under the genteel roof of Grandstone House, and beyond in the lane. When the words which claimed that Martha Oakes had seen her and left her in the freezing garden appeared on the board Lydie recalled Charlie's suspicion at the time of their search.

The alphabet now spelled out the question. 'Where is Charlie? Where is — ' Emily stopped short of indicating the letters that would spell — niece.

'Charlie's at headquarters trying to give some explanation but at present he knows less than we do,' Clive replied. 'But at least he'll be able to identify the American.' As gently as he could he told her of the accident in the lane. Then he asked her if she knew why her niece was out there at that time of night on the old bicycle and dressed in Martha Oakes's coat.

She shook her head and indicated the alphabet board. Moments later it displayed the letters, as available, get The AmErican. Both Clive and Lydie felt the emotion and fervour behind the words. Clive patted her hand and nodded reassuringly. He felt elated at the success of his idea that had made it possible for her to give them vital information and at the same time unburden herself. She had been unable to provide the surname of the American since he had been introduced only by his first name. For the present she had decided not to tell them of her discovery that the injured girl was not her niece at all. Sally Lane appeared to be an innocent victim who, when she recovered, would be asked to speak for herself. Later, by means of the alphabet board, she could tell Lydie, because Charlie must be told. The Will must be changed immediately.

Clive stood up. 'I'm going to headquarters with this information and with any luck should be able to bring Charlie back with me when I return. I shall have to stop off at the toy section in a department store to buy one of those.' He indicated the alphabet board. 'I have to return that one some time. I'll call in at the hospital again and I'll phone if there's any news. In the meantime Lydie if Emily remembers anything more that may be of help ring headquarters. I'll be back as soon as I possibly can.' He bent to kiss Lydie. 'Don't come down darling.'

Lydie nodded. 'Hurry back — and bring Charlie. I'll telephone the hospital shortly to enquire if there's been any improvement.'

As Clive Wessley went down the stairs he was pondering on what he had just learned about Martha Oakes. When he reached the hall he called, 'Martha I'd like a word please.' He went into the drawing room.

Moments later she was standing before him. He contemplated the granite-like features and wondered if she really was capable of such a callous act as Emily had claimed; if so with what motive? Inheritance? Often, over the years, he had been surprised that such obmutescence had been tolerated by Emily Penne; although Martha was undoubtedly an excellent housekeeper. But such a depressing, unfathomable presence! Now as he spoke he watched her face closely. 'According to Emily there are a few things you can tell me that may help with my enquiries regarding the events which took place here last evening.' To satisfy her questioning look he explained. 'We have found a way of communicating with her.' He decided to keep the method secret from her for the moment.

Coolly she stared back at him. But behind the impassive facade her mind was active, wondering what means he had found to get information from someone who had lost the power of speech. She wished now that she had followed behind him earlier to see for herself. If he thought he could intimidate her with his questions he was very much mistaken. She'd known him since he was a small boy, brought to the house by his mother to take tea with the Penneston-Barkleys. His Scotland Yard status carried no weight with her. She spoke now. 'It's understandable that the shock of what happened to her niece must have affected her mind. That and the stroke has affected her brain. It's quite obvious that her mind's gone.'

For a few moments he studied the inscrutable face without comment. Then he surprised her with his next question. 'I understand from George Hill that you called on him some while back to show him a newspaper cutting and photograph. You apparently thought it was a photo of Charlie.' Closely he observed her and saw that the question had brought the reaction he had hoped for and half expected.

A spark of life lit the dour expression and momentarily revealed her true feelings. 'It *is* him.' She almost spat the words out. 'Any fool could see it. A gaol-bird that's what he is. I told her but she wouldn't listen. Fanciful she called me! Yet I know she saw it too. She just didn't want to get rid of him. Likes the attention too much — his fussing over her. He's here for one thing only — her mon . . . '

Abruptly she broke off as if suddenly becoming aware that she had allowed her tongue too much freedom. She had broken her golden rule that she'd always been careful never to break. She had jumped at the opportunity which his receptive ears invited, to expose Charlie Barnes to someone who would listen. In succumbing she had let her customary barrier fall.

'Thank you Martha,' he especially refrained from giving the words the emphasis that he thought they merited as he left the house.

Minutes later he was driving through the village on his way back to town and headquarters with his latest information and hopefully to collect Charlie. After which he would buy a replacement alphabet and call in at the hospital with it. With any luck he might get to spend an hour or so of the Christmas holiday with Lydie. He somehow doubted it though.

19

CHRISTMAS EVE

In Berry Lane James Maddison opened the field-gate to drive the hired car through and over the frozen mud to park it behind the hedge out of sight of the road. As he got from the car he drew his top-coat collar up about his ears. Although barely six o'clock in the evening it was dark and the clear jewelled sky foretold a frosty night.

Returning to the lane he began a brisk walk in the direction of Grandstone House. In one gloved hand he held a flashlight, not switched on, the other strayed to his top-coat pocket and he fingered the hard outline of a revolver.

When he reached the house he kept to the shadows and made his way round to the back. His heavy breath misted on the frosty air in a shaft of light thrown from a downstairs window. Stealthily, keeping close to the wall he moved, trying doors and windows on the way. The French door to the sewing room gave to his touch as he turned the knob. The hinge made a faint squeak as the door moved inwards under his careful hand. He paused to listen for any response to the telltale sound.

Briefly he played the beam of the flashlight to show a clear path across the room to the inner door then switched off.

Leaving the French door open behind him he crossed the room. For fear of risking another give-away hinge he opened the door slowly. He paused again to listen. The downstairs hall-lights were on. Cautiously he moved across the marble floor towards the kitchen where he thought he would find the housekeeper. He saw the room was empty and cursed softly. He moved along to the other rooms downstairs; all were unlit. Moments later he stood at the base of the stairs looking up. Lights were on in the upper corridor and landing. His eyes searched for the light switch in the downstairs hall. He located and flicked it and left the hall in darkness. Slowly and silently he climbed the stairs.

In Emily Penne's bedroom Lydie's head nodded forward as much delayed sleep overtook her. The book from which she had been reading slipped from her lap to the carpeted floor with a soft thud which aroused her. She opened her eyes and blinked hard to stay awake.

With pillows for added comfort on the

chaise longue she had kept constant watch at the bedside throughout the night and day, leaving the room only to go to the bathroom and to the kitchen to prepare food and hot drinks. At present only the two of them were in the house. Clive Wessley and Charlie had as yet not returned.

Earlier Emily Penne, by means of the alphabet board, had given instructions to Lydie. She was to order Martha Oakes to leave the house and never return. Charlie would send a cheque to cover what wages she was owed when he returned.

This Lydie had done with pleasure and Martha Oakes had swept out claiming that she had intended to leave anyway rather than live under the same roof as a crook. To which Lydie, being thankful to see the back of her, had paid no heed.

The alphabet board had been put to constant use during the long hours of waiting for Clive and Charlie to appear. One message Lydie had found more startling than the rest. After much questioning and manoeuvring of the plastic characters on the board Lydie had transcribed the message onto the pad and re-read it back for confirmation of its substance. With frantic nods Emily Penne had assured her of its truth. She had looked worried at the doubts that showed on Lydie's face at first.

An hour ago Lydie had answered a telephone call from Scotland Yard headquarters with a message that Clive and Charlie would be back around six o'clock.

Still striving to shake off sleep she looked across to the bed and saw that Emily was wide awake. She went over and patted the hands that rested on the counterpane. They felt cold to touch. 'Shall I fetch another blanket?'

Emily Penne shook her head in reply. Lydie glanced at the china clock on the bureau. 'They'll be here soon Emily.' She seated herself on the bed and idly picked up the writing pad on which she had transcribed the messages. Alongside she had written her own thoughts on these. About to ask further questions now she changed her mind as she heard a familiar sound of the top stair creaking. She tensed — alert, her head to one side listening. Then she relaxed. 'It's all right. I locked the back and side doors myself and no one can get in the front without a key.'

Emily Penne had also heard the sound and with a concerned expression on her face was nodding towards the alphabet board.

Lydie went through the procedure once again of pointing to the letters which from

301

practice and understanding where there was a lack of available characters had become a speedier process. Moments later the message on the board read . . . sewing Rom dOr.

Lydie sprang up from the bed. 'I didn't check that one! I'll go down and . . . ' She saw that Emily Penne's eyes were staring fixedly on the partly open bedroom door as though some sixth sense had drawn them there.

The atmosphere in the room was taut as Lydie too stared at it. Then with a sudden movement she strode across the room and flung the door open wide.

She relaxed and turned to smile reassuringly, but saw that Emily Penne was once again indicating the board with her head.

Lydie returned to the bedside and under the directing nods spelled out the words . . . GUn burea. She had to think a bit about the second word before she worked out that it was meant to be bureau; the board lacking the third U.

Surprised she was about to brush aside such a drastic step. Then seeing the fear in the eyes of the old lady she went across to the bureau. After a little searching she found an old army revolver under a collection of yellowed documents. Hesitant to handle such an alien object she stared down at it for several seconds before picking it up. It looked clumsy in her delicate hands. Never in her life before had she even been close to firearms of any description let alone actually handled one. She wondered if it was loaded or merely bluff to deter an intruder. She glanced back at the bed and said, 'Don't worry Emily.' Then she left the room and made her way towards the stairs holding the revolver out ahead of her in both hands.

When she reached the landing she paused as she saw that the downstairs hall-lights were switched off. She was sure that she'd left these on. The large Roman copper light-fittings each carried five globes and the possibility that all ten had burned out simultaneously was too remote to be feasible. It was normal household practise to leave those lights on all evening to show the way from room to room. Switching them off late at night was the responsibility of the last person to retire. Fear gripped her now as she half turned to look behind. Her eyes travelled to each partly open door in turn. All the rooms except Emily Penne's were unlit. Someone could be lurking in any one of them. A sudden impulse to run back into the room she'd just left and lock the door almost overwhelmed her. She exerted her courage. Bracing herself she continued on down the stairs, lit only by the upstairs corridor lights. When she reached the hall she glanced towards the dark shadows as she made her way to the light-switch and flicked it. As light flooded the hall she hurried towards the sewing room. When she saw the partly open door her first thought was to lock it. Then common sense told her that someone had used it to enter the house. The faint hope she had nursed that the hall lights were off by her own omission, due to traumatic events, instantly vanished. No one in the household would have left a door open in this freezing weather. She closed the door but left it unlocked, then returned to the hall. She stood motionless, listening for any sounds. The faint squeak of a door hinge caught her ears and by reflex action she looked towards the upstairs landing and corridor. With a gasp she saw that the upstairs corridor was now in darkness. She made a dash for the stairs but before she reached them the downstairs lights were switched off. She stiffened as she hard the sound of someone breathing — quite close. Trying to judge distance in the darkness she moved forward towards the stairs. With her foot she felt for the bottom stair and with one hand on the banisters began to guide herself up. If she could just reach the bedroom and lock herself in with Emily.

Halfway up she took courage and looked behind her. 'Who are you, what do you want? Are you the beast — ' Suddenly she was caught in a flashlight. The gun in her hands showed up starkly as she held it out now at arms length and turned to face the intruder. 'I warn you — I shall not hesitate to shoot . . .'

'Nor I lady.' The tone of voice was cold and convincing and she knew that it was the American returned.

James Maddison was seething. Things had gone crazily wrong for him. If Sally Lane died the Oakes bitch would have no reason to keep her mouth shut, for there would be no inheritance to share. Disposing of her would of course take the heat off the Baines guy who at present, being in police custody, had the best alibi in the world. But there was no other course now. Where the goddamn hell was the bitch? He had come back to Grandstone House with the express purpose of dealing with her. He hadn't expected to discover that the old lady had survived either. But she couldn't tell tales, so didn't pose any threat.

Before switching on the flashlight he had pulled a scarf up to screen the lower half of his face.

Lydie squinting in the bright spotlight

backed slowly up the stairs — feeling for each tread with the back of her heels. The brilliant light in her eyes prevented her from seeing his features.

Relentlessly he kept the ray full on her as she made her way up but made no attempt to follow.

Rapidly her mind worked as she tried to make the split second decision . . . which room? Emily's or Charlie's? To protect the old lady — or warn the men of the American's presence when they arrived. Emily's room overlooked the back of the property and warning the men would not be possible. Charlie's room overlooked the front driveway. From his window she could call out to let them know in advance that an intruder — a madman wielding a gun was in the house. Remembering the creak of the stair she had heard earlier she knew that already he had been upstairs. Surely if he intended to harm Emily he would have acted then.

By the time she reached the landing she had made her choice. Turning she fled into Charlie's room locking the door behind her. She dashed across to the window and leaned out, oblivious to the icy blast around her face and shoulders. All was still and silent as she listened for the distant sound of an approaching car in the lane which would tell her that they were arriving. Leaving the window open she recrossed the room and stood at the door listening. No sound came from upstairs or below. Cautiously she opened the door a crack. Only a shaft of light from the still partly open door of Emily Penne's room lit the darkness. Easing the door open further she slipped out and dashed across to the lighted room and darted in, closing and locking the door behind her.

Emily Penne started a frantic mumbling and attempted to raise her hand to point. Even in this fear-laden moment Lydie noticed that the movement was stronger than it had been earlier. 'Did you see him Emily?' She payed close attention to the response. When the nodded reply came she asked, 'Was it the American?' Again she saw the nod which confirmed that the intruder had been upstairs while she was checking the sewing room door. 'Listen Emily. I'm going into Charlie's room so that I can call out the window and warn them when they arrive. They should be here soon now. Will you be afraid if I leave you?'

Emily Penne shook her head, more vigorously now. 'Good. Don't worry. I'll close your door. If he intended to harm us he'd have done so by now.' Not entirely believing this she gave the old hand a comforting squeeze. Anyone who committed such a cold-blooded act as he already had was capable of anything. She slipped out again closing the door behind her this time and hurried back to Charlie's room. As she stepped inside and reached for the light switch she was grabbed from behind and pulled roughly into the centre of the room. 'Where's that damned housekeeper?' he demanded. 'And don't try bluffing me or calling out. I know there's no one in the house besides you and the old girl.'

'Martha Oakes is no longer employed here. What do you want with her anyway?' Even as she asked the question the answer struck her. 'She's not the only person who can identify you. Charlie can and . . . Paula.' She had hesitated before speaking the name, still unsure whether Emily's mind had wandered to the point of fantasy in believing that her visitor was an impostor as she'd claimed in the alphabet message.

In the darkness he gave a stiff smile believing that the housekeeper, still hopeful of Sally Lane's recovery, had not as yet exposed the bogus niece.

As Lydie struggled to free herself from his grip he shook her roughly and demanded, 'Where is she?'

'I don't know.' She felt the side of the bed

against the back of her legs. As she struggled they both overbalanced onto the bed and she felt the touch of cold metal when the gun contacted her cheek as they fell.

Although he had not switched on his flashlight she knew that he must still be carrying it on him since it was not in his hand. Momentarily her arm was released and she instantly reached into the pocket of his top-coat. Luckily she chose right first time, for there wouldn't be a second chance. Her hand closed over the torch and in one quick movement she drew it out. Taking him unawares she switched it on and shone it full into his face at close-quarters.

He cursed and put his hand to his eyes to shield them from the blinding glare, and as he did this her other arm was momentarily released. The scarf had slipped from his face in the struggle. As he brought his hand down to wrest the torch from her a car pulled up noisily in the driveway and his hand went instantly to her mouth. The arm holding her down was like a steel vice. In the hand which was pinned down she still held the revolver. She tried to pull the trigger to warn the men but it was too stiff and would require both hands to manipulate. Instead she switched the torch on and off repeatedly until he knocked it from her hand. To do this he was obliged to remove his hand from her mouth. Before he could clamp it back she screamed loudly.

The moment the car pulled up outside the house Charlie remarked, 'That's strange — the hall light isn't on! Lydie must . . . ' He stopped short as he saw the quick flashes lighting his bedroom window.

Simultaneously he and Clive Wessley had looked up. At that same moment they heard the scream. Both scrambled from the car and sprinted to the front entrance. On finding the doors locked Charlie felt in his pocket for the key, before remembering that he'd not taken it with him. 'Quick — round the back,' he gasped.

Moments later, having found the unlocked door, they sprinted up the stairs together three at a time and burst into the bedroom. Charlie switched on the light. Clive Wessley rushed at the American but halted as he was confronted with the gun.

'Keep back.' Although the hand that held the revolver was steady enough his eyes were like those of a trapped wild animal; those of the two he held at bay were calculating and wary.

Released, Lydie got to her feet. James Maddison paid no heed to her now, as if he suddenly found her of no consequence, no threat.

At no time in his entire life had he felt genuine affection for anyone. As a child he had received none. No example had been set for him. His stripper-whore mother had inflicted a variety of temporary and indifferent step-fathers on his young life. In consequence he had grown up believing that love was a non-existent state outside movies and silly books; merely a charade written about to make money. He could not consider the possible sacrifice one person will make for another.

Lydie's eyes travelled from the gun in his hand to the two motionless but threatening giants who stood baring the way between himself and escape. She knew for sure that Clive Wessley would never allow this wild-eyed American to escape the law. Either he or Charlie would be shot and likely killed in the process. Bluff was no part of this scene.

'Move away from that door,' James Maddison commanded taking a step closer to them.

Without hesitation Lydie flung herself upon him. As she came he swung round and fired the gun.

In that instant Charlie rushed forward and dealt a crashing blow with his fist that brought the American down to the floor where he lay senseless.

311

A split second behind Charlie, Clive Wessley moved and bent over to snap handcuffs on the unresisting wrists before picking up the revolver.

He heard the strangled cry of alarm as Charlie sank to his knees beside Lydie as she fell to the floor.

Grim faced Clive went out into the corridor and as he telephoned for an ambulance placed the revolver alongside the phone on a small Chippendale table.

He then made a call to Scotland Yard Headquarters. 'Get two men here quickly Joe,' his voice was broken and strained as he explained briefly what had taken place. Hastily he replaced the receiver and returned to the bedroom. On the threshold he halted and his words mingled with those of Charlie as he said, 'I've called an ambulance.'

As though from a deep pit he heard Charlie's voice. 'Oh God Lyd! Tell me what to do! Tell me . . . '

Lydie's fast-dulling eyes were focussed on Charlie's face. He was like a helpless little boy — pleading. She fought to keep her eyes from closing and her voice was barely a whisper. 'I love you Charlie . . . be good.'

'No — no — no . . . Lydie! Don't leave me!' A sob separated the appeals. 'I can't live without you Lydie!'

Her voice was barely a whisper before it trailed off . . . 'You will Charlie . . . '

As her eyes closed on the last word he leaned across her limp body. His voice was a hoarse slow motion of anguish and despair. 'No Lydie — no . . . no . . . no . . . '

In the doorway Clive Wessley stood — an onlooker — too stunned for the present to make any further movement. Then as if taking a physical blow his tall body sagged and he caught his breath in quick gasps. Suddenly an old man he propelled himself stiffly forward until he was looking down upon the waxen face cradled in the arms of Charlie. With a wooden motion he reached out to touch the hunched shoulder — but his hand remained motionless above the Harris tweed. Time stood still and the words which his emotion choked voice could not release never reached the ears of Charlie.

Slowly his hand fell away and he turned steely eyes on James Maddison who was struggling to sit up. An expression of pure loathing settled on his face now as he towered over him and spoke slowly in tones as cold as the night frost. 'You — low — life — bastard. You'll — pay — for — this.'

Shrinking back the American flinched under the menacing words which came like pistol shots hitting him between the eyes. He was dragged roughly to his feet by the back of his collar and pushed from the room into the corridor and towards the top of the stairs. 'Kneel down you scum.' Clive Wessley ordered, forcing him to his knees. With a key from his pocket he released one bracelet of handcuffs and thrust the free hand around the heavy newel-post before securing it again in the manacle. Having done this he went to the telephone once again and without taking his flint-like eyes from his prisoner except to briefly dial he spoke in an emotion choked voice. 'Clive Wessley again Joe. Make that murder, and tell them to hurry before they have another on their hands.' As he replaced the receiver he remembered Emily and went into her room. He found her struggling to lever herself from the bed, her eyes fixed on the wheelchair close by.

When she saw him her eyes pleaded for him to tell her what had been happening outside her room. He went across to assist her. 'Charlie is all right Emily. We have the American handcuffed. I've sent for help.' He paused to gather courage to continue. But at first the words resisted and stuck in his throat. 'Lydie — Lydie — he shot her . . . she's . . . ' He finished what had to be said but the word was lost in a sob.

Emily Penne had not needed the words.

She could see by his expression. Her look of distress showed that she had understood. Breathing hard now she pointed with a distinct movement towards the wheelchair.

He would rather that she stayed where she was for the present but, although engulfed in his own misery, could see that she was clearly determined. To restrain her in her precarious state could prove fatal.

With ease he lifted her into the wheelchair. Immediately she set about trying to move it towards the door and again succeeded in raising her hand to point.

Understanding he pushed the chair out into the corridor and placed it beside the telephone table. On no account would he take her into Charlie's room. Next he went downstairs to unlock the front door and open it slightly so that the ambulance men could admit themselves on arrival. Not that speed mattered now.

After switching on the front porch-lights and the lights downstairs he returned to Charlie's room and sat down heavily on the bed. His head bent forward he buried his face in his hands.

Charlie was still cradling the body of Lydie in his arms as he rocked to and fro completely immersed in an abyss of grief and regret.

Out on the landing James Maddison, still on his knees, looked away from the bitter loathing in the old eyes fixed upon him only a few feet away. The arm of the wheelchair was on a level with the telephone table where Clive Wessley had placed the revolver taken from the American.

Emily Penne turned her eyes now to the gun which was within her reach. Gradually her right hand moved towards it. Contempt for the kneeling man lent power and determination to her afflicted arm. Her hand closed around the cold steel and dragged it across the smooth polished surface toward her. She felt its weight as it slid off the edge of the table onto the arm of the wheelchair then down onto her thigh where it lay half hidden by the folds of her knitted bed-shawl.

Using her elbow for leverage she pushed against the table and sent the chair forward. It stopped less than two feet from the kneeling man where he was slumped against the banister posts.

At the movement so close he turned disinterested eyes upon her.

Now, as her hand moved, the corner of her shawl fell aside revealing the grey metal of his own gun.

Even before the look of surprise registered on his face the first shot was discharged.

316

Emily Penne fired the gun twice. The first bullet struck the newel post; the second found its target.

As if split second decision had told him that his back was less vulnerable he had turned his body and the bullet pierced his heart from behind.

At the sound of the first shot Clive Wessley raised his head from his hands. But it was several seconds before he could return his full senses to the living world.

As he jumped to his feet the second shot was fired. He reached the doorway in time to see the American slump against the banisters. At once he took in the situation and knelt to feel the pulse of the manacled wrist. He felt none. Reproachfully now he turned to the old lady, 'You let him off too lightly Emily.'

The loud clanging of a bell announced the arrival of the ambulance as it entered the driveway.

Motionless he stood until the men came into the hall. As they came up the stairs he took a key from his pocket and unlocked the cuffs to remove them from the dead man's wrists. For the next few minutes he had no time to wonder at the borrowed strength with which the gun had been operated. Now, as he turned to move the wheelchair back the revolver slid from cold hands as the final stroke seized Emily Penne and her head slumped forward onto her chest. Into her frail hands she had taken the law, purposely to dispense a wild justice in which she had been judge and executioner. Her last thoughts had been of loathing coupled with fear that an inconsistent British justice system might not exact a high enough penalty from the monster at her feet.

Nowadays they would not demand his worthless life for taking that of lovely innocent Lydie.

20

CHRISTMAS DAY

Without awareness Charlie's eyes followed the descent of an ethereal snowflake as it hovered imponderable before surrendering to gravity and extinction on the window sill. From the window seat in the drawing room he had watched the gradual lightening of the dawn sky.

In the early hours Clive Wessley had driven him back to the house from police headquarters where they had been to give an account of the murders. On the way he had offered the hospitality of Tanglewood for the next few days to spare a return to the scene so recently scarred by tragedy.

But Charlie had preferred to be alone with his grief. They could be of no comfort to each other. Each would carry his own separate burden. In the cold silence he sat, still stunned by shock and disbelief. The fire had long since burned out and he still wore his top-coat. He turned his eyes from the window and looked across at the lifeless ashes in the fire grate. All dead. Everything dead. Like the ashes he felt dead. His spirit was dead. There seemed no purpose to his life any more. Someone had once told him, 'You don't know what happiness is until you lose it.' Well he knew the truth of this now. He had thought himself happy in his materialistic outlook on life. Why had he been so blind? Why had he not seen? There never had been a time when Lydie was not in his life. He had taken her for granted all those years. Never could he have imagined life without her — a world without her in it. In his mind he kept hearing her last words when he'd told her that he couldn't live without her. 'You will Charlie . . . you will . . .'

His head slumped forward in his hands, while his anguished heart did it's futile crying, inconsolable.

A thin layer of snow covered the lawns and shrubs now. An hour had passed since he'd watched the first snowflake float past the window panes. Memories of his childhood with Lydie had filled his thoughts. Recollections only twisted the knife in his heart at present. Cold, yet not feeling it, he stood gazing disinterestedly about him. He was thinking of that day when he had first come to Grandstone House. A million years ago it seemed like instead of merely nine months. He remembered well his elation at finding

320

exactly the kind of place he had always hankered for. Through different eyes now he saw it all. How could he have considered it to be the most important thing in his life when, he realised now, Lydie had been. Material possessions counted for nothing in the scheme of things . . . the truly important things . . . the worthwhile precious things.

Greed had motivated murder to be committed in this house. And for some as yet unknown reason a girl lay in hospital lucky to have survived an attempt on her life. As the direct result of these deeds a sweet old lady had died, her swan-song a criminal act to avenge the death of Lydie. In her heart as it stopped had been hate for the man she wanted wiped from the face of the earth.

He turned again to look out of the window. To his left he could see the bare branches outlined with a coating of snow. Like the bright blooms of summer Lydie had gone. But the roses would bloom again — and he'd have no heart to watch them now. Listless he left the room. In the hall he paused beside the undecorated Christmas tree. He stared at the rich green foliage. Eons ago it seemed he had brought it back from the village, intending to decorate it on Christmas eve. On his return he had found the American already in the house. Little had they known then what the madman was planning.

His mind recalled the previous Christmas which he had spent in prison. He remembered the words in a letter which he'd written to Lydie . . . 'We'll make up for it next Christmas Lyd . . . you can bet your life on it.'

With a sob he turned away from the tree. With a slow heavy tread he went up the stairs.

Since they had taken the body of Lydie away he had not entered his room. Now outside the door he paused. Sometime he would have to go in and collect his belongings and move them to another room. He put out his hand to open the door — but let it drop away. Not yet — he couldn't go in just yet.

He moved along to Emily Penne's room. The door was open. He entered. The bed was still dishevelled. The alphabet board was where Lydie had left it but now partly obscured by the bed-covers. This was the first he had seen of it. Clive Wessley had explained its purpose to him when they were at police headquarters and had related the information already gained from Emily by its means. Idly curious Charlie put out his hand to uncover it and was startled by its last message, still displayed . . . GUn burea. The unfinished word was obvious, the missing letter due to the fact that the alphabet contained only two sets of characters.

He reached out to straighten the covers and the pad which Lydie had used to transcribe the messages fell to the floor. He bent to pick it up and recognising the handwriting stared blankly at it knowing that these were the last words she ever wrote. They seemed to leap out, sparking his full attention to their substance. The girl is not my niece. Her name is Sally Lane. She came in Paula's place. Paula dead. Shot in New York after girl Lane had left. Martha knows. She listened in when American phoned. She arranged for his visit here.'

Charlie's brows drew together as he read and re-read the startling message.

He turned the page on the pad and read . . . 'The following is an account of information as given by Emily by means of the alphabet board. I have questioned her on the surprising claim and am absolutely certain she believes that the girl who is here on a visit is not her niece Paula, that her name is Sally Lane who came here in Paula's place. Emily claims to have discovered that her niece was shot and killed in New York after Sally Lane had left. But Sally did not know of this until the American telephoned her here, much later, to tell her the news.

Martha Oakes apparently overheard their conversation and made this known to Sally Lane. To do this she came into Emily's room believing that she could not be heard by Emily. She was obviously unaware that the hearing-aid which had been out for repair had been returned and that Emily was wearing it. Emily heard Martha call the girl Sally Lane. From what Emily told me by means of the alphabet board — her niece Paula had asked the girl Sally Lane to come on a visit in her place. In view of Emily's affliction from the recent stroke and awful experience last night I don't know what to make of it all. But she does appear to be in full possession of her faculties, and some explanation has to be found for the rest of events. Even so, surely if her niece had been killed wouldn't she, as next of kin, have been notified? I did suggest this to Emily but she's as mystified as I am.

Charlie let the page fall back into place as something started to tease his memory. But his grief-dulled mind could not for the present lift aside the obscuring curtain.

* * *

In Nightingale Hospital Sally Lane's eyelids flickered several times as she tried to focus through a mist onto the filmy curtains at the window of the private ward. Unblinking her eyes moved slowly around the room until they came to rest on Charlie seated at the bedside.

Suddenly summoning a smile of reassurance to his reluctant lips he leaned forward. But there was no response from the violet eyes resting on him.

A ward nurse presently reading the chart notes attached to the foot of the bed saw the movement and with an exclamation of delight hurried out to inform the ward doctor, and to page Clive Wessley who had recently left the room to fetch sandwiches and tea for himself and Charlie for they had been at the bedside for the last two hours.

As the mist before her eyes cleared Sally Lane stared vacantly at Charlie, her lips moving slightly, without sound.

'Hello. It's Charlie here. How are you feeling now?'

Again her lips moved silently until at last her voice, strained and weak, became audible. 'Where — what . . . ?'

'Don't try to talk yet.'

A small frown appeared on her brow just beneath the bandages. 'I don't . . . ' her voice trailed off and her eyes closed again.

'Just rest. You're going to be fine,' he said

gently. He felt a deep responsibility for her now and intended to give her all the help and support he possibly could until she was well enough for him to leave her.

The doctor and nursing sister came hurrying in. Charlie left the room. He went to sit in the corridor where he was joined almost immediately by Clive Wessley carrying a tray with food and drink for them.

21

NEW YEARS DAY

The two funerals were now behind him. Both Lydie and Emily Penneston-Barkley had been buried in the small churchyard in the grounds of the little village church. This had been packed to capacity for the service, and outside, the lane lined with the overflow of local people who had come to pay their last respects. Although they had not seen Emily Penne about in the village since the death of her husband they remembered her friendly nature, with no hint of snobbery about her, despite her wealth. The news of the shootings and consequent death of the young visitor to Grandstone House had been a great shock to the small local community. Nothing like it had ever happened before, at least in their lifetime, in the village of Redcliffe. And on top of that the accident in the lane, still a mystery to them all, had aroused much curiosity and speculation. The only person among them who could throw any light upon it had kept silent. And even she had been shocked at the events which had taken place after her forced departure from the house.

A few of Lydie's colleagues from the hospital had travelled to Redcliffe to attend her funeral, but still shocked and upset themselves had not imposed on Charlie's privacy and grief by visiting the house after the service was over.

The family lawyer had attended. Afterwards he returned to the house purposely to carry out his instructions which was to read the last will and testament of Emily Penneston-Barkley. He was presently in the drawing room with Charlie and Martha Oakes having previously arranged the meeting.

'This shouldn't take long since there are only three beneficiaries,' he said, seating himself at a circular mahogany table. From his briefcase he took some documents which he placed before him. He adjusted his spectacles. 'Mr Baines — or is it Barnes?' Emily didn't write the name too clearly.' He glanced up briefly and regarded the abstracted gaze of Charlie as he replied disinterestedly, 'Barnes.'

'There are two other beneficiaries.' His eyes travelled to Martha Oakes who sat stiff backed and keenly receptive although impassive outwardly, except for the slight twist that formed on her lips when Charlie had stated his correct name.

The lawyer continued, 'It is most unfortunate that Emily's niece cannot be with us at present. But I understand that her condition has improved and that she is now off the danger list.' He paused again to give a cursory glance at the documents before him and rubbed his hands together for warmth. The room was cold and no fire had been lit. His eyes rested on Charlie. 'You look as though you'd be all the better for a drink. All right with you if I fetch one? I know where it's kept. I used to be a frequent dinner guest here when William was alive. He and Emily were my friends as well as my clients.'

Without waiting for a reply from Charlie he left the room and minutes later returned with three glasses of Madeira on a silver tray which he handed round.

Vacantly Charlie stared down at the drink before picking it up.

The lawyer raised his glass and proposed a toast. 'To the complete recovery of Miss Carpenter.'

Martha Oakes raised her glass reluctantly but said nothing.

Charlie did likewise but with a slight nod of agreement. Where was the point in wishing recovery for *Miss Carpenter* when, if the message Lydie had transcribed from the alphabet board was to be believed, she apparently was already dead.

As he swallowed the wine, and the lawyer spoke the name Paula Carpenter, the words — the girl is not my niece Paula is dead, were drawn to the surface of his mind. He had no interest in either the inheritance or the lawyer, he just wanted him gone; and the sour-faced ex-housekeeper with him, as much as he would have liked to question her on what she knew. And he thought she knew plenty. She had kept her lips clamped during police questioning according to Clive Wessley.

Charlie became aware that his name was being spoken. ' . . . to Charlie Barnes I leave Grandstone House, its entire contents and the estate on which it stands . . . '

Unmoved Charlie heard the words which, barely a week ago, would have left him elated. But a week ago was a world away in time, from which he had retreated in the embrace of his despond.

As the voice continued speaking a phrase or word now and then penetrated his indifferent ears. 'In the event of . . . niece Paula . . . death without issue all . . . pass to Charlie . . . ' The wry smile that wanted to reach his lips could not surface from beneath his misery. Yes — a week ago the words would have been music to his ears. But now — he couldn't give a bloody damn.

* ★ *

The lawyer had left. Martha Oakes, face more sour than ever, had left. Charlie had not even made a move to see them out.

On the window seat in the drawing room again he sat staring out at the garden. A fine mist hung over the silent scene. The weather was turning milder and thawing the earlier frost. Listless, at present no direction in his life, he felt an impatience to leave the house. Memories here were too painful to be endured and the waiting interminable. But wait he must — until the new mistress of Grandstone House was fit to leave Nightingale Hospital. A big problem existed with regards to this. He recalled the words of the hospital doctor. 'She is still suffering from memory loss, and this may continue for some time. Very hard to predict. Perhaps when she is back on familiar ground with familiar surroundings there is every chance she may remember. One can't hurry these matters or say with any certainty. Some similar cases have taken years, others not long, some never. Each patient is individual. Look on the bright side, she survived the injuries, that's the most important thing for the present.'

The familiar sound of the brass letterbox flap roused him from his thoughts and he

331

went out into the hall to collect the post. One letter lay on the floor. For a few moments he stared down at it before bending to pick it up. The words — Return to sender — were scrawled across the front of the envelope which looked much travelled. It bore three different postmarks, two of which were clear. New York and Redcliffe. But all dates were indistinct. He turned the envelope over to read the name of the sender on the back. S. Lane — Grandstone House Berry Lane Redcliffe England.

Instantly a chord in his memory struck. That name Lane . . . Lydie had written it on the pad in her account of the alphabet messages transcribed from the board.

He hadn't mentioned it to Clive Wessley or the police. There seemed little point with the girl lying seriously injured in hospital and the possibility that she might not survive. Also the revelation had been pushed to the back of his mind by his own personal grief and wretchedness. In any event at the time of reading it he had considered it too absurd to merit serious thought, and no doubt the wanderings of an afflicted mind. Yet, from events, he now realised that the mind of Emily Penne had not been impaired by the stroke at all. And this returned letter was further proof that her wits were as sharp as ever to the end. Who then was the girl in Nightingale Hospital? According to the messages on the pad — Martha Oakes knew — and certainly the American had.

Absently he drummed his fingers against the underside of the envelope as he re-read the name and pondered on who exactly was Sally Lane. For the present even she herself didn't know.

As he stood considering the letter he pursed his lips in indecision. Then suddenly he strode across to the hall table, took up a silver-handled letter opener and slit open the envelope. He returned to the window-seat and unfolded the sheets of notepaper to read . . .

Dear Paula

I have waited a while before writing just as you advised me to. Already I'm quite settled in at Grandstone House and have been accepted as you. No one suspects that I'm not. I must admit that I had second thoughts when I got to the airport, especially as you were unable to be there to see me off. I almost turned back on the way — all the while I was thinking . . . they'll be sure to see through me instantly. But your aunt is such a sweet lady and so happy to welcome me. I honestly can't figure why you've never wanted to come here. The house is just wonderful — beautiful. I'd like to stay here permanently — oh how I wish I could. I do feel bad about deceiving your aunt like this. But I have the consolation that this visit made her very happy — so where is the harm really — so long as she believes that I'm you. That's all that really matters for the moment isn't it. You have misjudged both your aunt and Charlie in believing that he is trying to usurp you. He's no threat to your inheritance. He's not the scheming kind you suspected him to be. He is a perfect English gentleman and I can't begin to describe his looks! Honey — is he handsome! You have missed out by not coming yourself. You would never look twice at James again. The worst of it all — for you at any rate — is that you'll never be able to visit your aunt again — not ever — had you realised that or thought about it when you asked me to come in your place? You'll never be able to see your aunt again. That's sad. We look alike honey but not to such an extent as that. I can only say that I wish she were my aunt. And you'll never be able to meet Charlie now either. Just think — he might well have been your destiny and you surely would have grown to love this old house and the estate. The countryside here is wonderful and I hate the thought of returning to noisy old New York. I wish Charlie could be my destiny. As if I could be so lucky. He has taken me up to London town a couple of times at your aunt's suggestion. As you know my life-long ambition has been to see London. I loved it, especially with Charlie as my escort. I feel positively guilty for enjoying myself so much at your expense Paula honey. But remember it was all your idea — well yours and James's. I'm glad now that he talked me into it. Although of course, as already said, I hate deceiving your aunt. When you write to me don't forget to type the envelope because your aunt might recognise your handwriting. But then I'm sure you will have already thought of that. So long for now.

Love Sally L.

Brows drawn Charlie looked up from the pages of pale-grey Basildon Bond; the written contents substantiated what Lydie had written on the pad.

Quite suddenly he recalled what it was that had eluded his memory at the time of reading the messages transcribed by Lydie. It was the daily switching of the cutlery which at every meal had always been laid out by Martha Oakes for a left handed diner in the place where their guest sat. In turn this brought to mind the letter which he had read from the bundle in the bureau the day when Emily had fallen asleep in the garden . . . something about tennis and being left-handed. It was beginning to tie in. If this part of the transcribed messages from the alphabet board proved true — then surely so must the rest of the information be reliable. Martha Oakes did know more than she was telling. Not that she'd had much to say anyway. But she must have withheld information. Why hadn't she informed Clive Wessley? Why would she stay silent and allow an impostor to inherit? Surely not merely to spite himself! The letter in his hands explained a lot — but there was still much to be uncovered.

Taking the letter with him he went upstairs to the bedroom used by Sally Lane. For a while he stood looking about him hoping to find something which might offer further information — some clue.

He crossed the room to a small oak bedside cabinet and opened the top drawer. Inside he found a red leather writing case. He unzipped this. It contained writing paper and envelopes which matched the letter. He recalled now that she had bought this in London on their first trip there together. In any case he was in no doubt whatever that she was the writer of the letter in his hand.

He moved aside the other items in the drawer and exposed a large crimson and gold bound diary. It looked expensive and its size obviously designed for those who wish to keep a full and detailed account of their days. It held no key in its gold lock. After a search of the drawer he found the key wrapped in a silk handkerchief. He stood motionless holding the key in one hand and the diary in the other, vaguely aware of the ornamental china clock on the dressing-table ticking away the minutes while he contemplated the ethics of his proposed intention. It was imperative that he know more about the girl in Nightingale Hospital for at present she knew nothing about herself.

The decision made he seated himself on the bed and with the tiny gold key unlocked the recent past of Sally Lane. He turned first to the last pages, since these were most relevant. He flicked the pages to find the entry made for the day on which the letter had been written. He was concerned only with any reference to its contents. The days had been recorded in small neat handwriting. Every fraction of space provided for each day was filled, giving the impression that no event in the daily life of the writer passed as unworthy of storing in cobalt-blue ink for future reference.

Ten minutes later he glanced up from the pages which had told him the story from the day the letter had been written, up until December 23rd. Those final recorded daily accounts could not tell him what she had been doing out in Berry Lane in the freezing weather on the old upright and wearing the black coat which belonged to Martha Oakes only minutes after the American had left the house. Nor why he had returned. This was left to his own conjecture. He had read the reason why the American had come to the house. He had worked out for himself that the scheming housekeeper had twice escaped murderous hands and in her place Sally Lane had been the victim, almost killed, perhaps permanently impaired. And worse . . . his own sweet innocent Lydie had died. There could be only one reason why Martha Oakes was staying silent, biding her time. She still hoped to gain from the legacy left to Sally Lane . . . probably had blackmail in mind.

His eyes skimmed once more over the neat entries . . .

Knowing James Maddison as I do I find it strange that he should be taking Martha Oakes' threat of blackmail so calmly, especially considering his angry outburst when I first told him that she had eavesdropped on his telephone calls to me . . .

Charlie turned back the pages and continued to read . . .

So many awful things have happened today. Martha Oakes eavesdropped on James and myself talking in the summer house. She has insisted that I arrange for him to come to the house to discuss what she heard. Must be blackmail she has in mind or she would have already exposed us to Emily. She came into Emily's room to tell me that she knew about my switch with Paula for the visit. Emily — thank heaven — was asleep and her hearing-aid out for repair as Martha well knew. But for all that it didn't seem right for her to confront me there with Emily present, even if she was asleep and couldn't hear. Then Charlie returned from the village and before he came upstairs I ran into my own room. I was still too shocked at what Martha Oakes had said and in no fit state to see Charlie

339

just then. Then I heard him telephoning the doctor. I ran back to Emily's room and could see that she'd had a seizure. I'd left her only a minute before and am sure she was asleep then. This stroke was more serious than her previous one. At present she is completely paralysed in her limbs and has lost her power of speech. I guess now that I shall never be able to tell her about the death of dear Paula, and the truth about myself. Or that Paula was my half sister — that we had the same father. Perhaps I never would have been able to anyway because it would have been cruel and the shock too much for her. I dearly wish that I could tell her that I meant no harm by the deceit — she never would have seen Paula again in any case. I know that she never would have come on a visit. I would so much have liked to have confided in Charlie — told him the truth — I don't think he would have forgiven me though for deceiving Emily. He is genuinely fond of her. But when the inheritance comes to me — as Paula — I shall make everything over to him — at least everything that is left after the two vultures Martha Oakes and James have grasped all they can. I shall have some explaining to do to Charlie because no doubt he is aware of the exact financial aspect of the estate. *Today on the stairs I almost confessed to him. I so desperately need someone to confide in, but I was afraid to. It's almost more than I can bear alone. I wish I could think that it would make no difference to his opinion of me if I explained the truth behind it all. But I feel that it would be expecting too much. I have no one at all. I belong nowhere now. My own identity was taken from me by James without my knowledge. I had no choice in the matter because I was not there when he buried Paula in my name. He never even contacted me to let me know that she had been shot and killed by his wife just after my plane had left New York, not until a few weeks after it happened.*

Having read this far and now enlightened to a greater extent Charlie turned back the pages to an earlier date in the diary and his fingers arrested a page which read . . .

How lonely I feel now that dear Paula is dead, and only two years after our discovering that we are half-sisters. I feel as if I have no one in the whole world now. Uncle and Aunt Macey don't count because I've never met them. They live so far away from New York and they are really only names mentioned to me by my mother. She didn't know them either. James must have remembered that I once mentioned this or he wouldn't have dared falsely identify Paula's body in my name, for he wouldn't be sure whether a relative might show up and want to view the body. As things were only he was required to do that, apart from those involved in the criminal investigation aspect of it all. How morbid this all is to record. Of one thing I am quite certain — he did not do it to protect me from prosecution for using Paula's passport for reasons of impersonating her. I'm afraid of his real motives. I shall know soon no doubt . . .

Charlie sighed and shook his head in disbelief even though he believed. He closed the diary having decided that he had read enough for the present. At least some of the mystery had now been explained. And at present he knew more about the girl in Nightingale Hospital than she knew herself. Perhaps, for the time being, her memory loss was a blessing after all. These recorded chronicles must lie dormant for the present — held in abeyance perhaps for an eternity; who could tell? Her very recent past, which had been linked up with his own life and Emily's in this house, was now suspended in time along with all that had gone before. As things were now would she, if she could, choose to forget? he wondered as he put aside the diary.

He picked up the returned letter and envelope and crossed the room to open the window. From his pocket he took a box of matches, struck one. He held the lighted flame to a corner of the pale-grey paper which held the clue to the past of the girl with a missing memory in Nightingale Hospital. Only when the flames licked at his fingers did he leave go. He watched the frangible black fragments float, light as thistledown, into the fine drizzling rain and disintegrate to merge with extinction. He closed the window and returned his attention to the diary. Those last recorded chronicles were not his to destroy. Good or bad they were an invaluable link that she might some day need when or if her memory returned. As things were, when she returned to the house which was her only home now, she would see the written evidence there — outside her powers of recall. Almost certainly she would doubt her own motives in the affair, and being a stranger to herself might surrender to the authorities. That would be additional mental trauma when she most needed peace of mind if she was to recover her memory. *If*. There was no guarantee that she would.

He re-locked the diary and stood thinking. After ten minutes deliberation he went back downstairs, into the library where he sat at the desk. From one of the drawers he took out a large manila envelope on which he wrote a message. He then enclosed the diary and the key in the envelope and sealed it. From a set of keys on the desktop he selected one and unlocked the top left-hand drawer. He transferred the contents to the one below. In the vacated drawer he deposited the diary locked the drawer and attached the key to his own personal set in a leather key-wallet which he carried in his pocket. From a spare set of household keys, kept high up in a recess of the carved architrave of the large built-in bookcase which stretched along an entire wall, he removed its twin. This too he attached to the key-ring in the wallet with his own set. Only those informed knew of the duplicate sets of keys kept in the recess which was not visible from the ground level. These were kept there in the event of emergency or loss.

He sat down on the leather couch to consider how best to set about finding someone to take his place with the garden maintenance. Also a woman to take on the position as housekeeper and prepare things ready for the return of the new mistress when she was released from the hospital.

22

In Nightingale Hospital Martha Oakes stared impassively down at the pale sleeping face. The nursing sister warned, 'She won't know you. She must be kept quiet and not be hassled in anyway about her memory loss.'

'Will she recover her memory?'.

'Impossible to predict. With absolute rest and quiet she may. Some do. Some don't. Each case is different. Just be thankful that she is recovering well from her physical injuries. We must be optimistic about the rest.' The nursing sister smiled and left the room.

Martha Oakes had come only out of curiosity to see for herself if it were really true that the girl was recovering well except from the amnesia state. This much she had been told when she telephoned to enquire. She had studied the newspaper accounts of the case and kept her own mouth shut tightly. She was well aware that Clive Wessley had not been satisfied with the little information she had given him. Well, he could think what the hell he liked. When he had questioned her about the search for Emily Penne who had been left to freeze in the garden she had denied emphatically that she'd seen her in the torch-beam. Nobody could prove otherwise.

These thoughts were running through her mind as her compassionless gaze rested on the pale silent face. Despite uncertain medical views she felt confident that this was not the end of her own schemes. This impostor from America would one day recover her past.

Abruptly now she turned away from the silent bed and left the hospital.

23

It seemed to Charlie as if history was repeating itself as he drove her for the second time a stranger through the gates of Grandstone House.

From Nightingale Hospital he had collected her in the Bentley. She was unaware that this was the car which had run her down in the lane; the scar on its front bumper, caused by the impact with the old upright, had been erased at the local garage workshop: Unlike the vivid scar still staining one side of her forehead. That would take time.

He glanced sideways at her, half expecting that some familiar sight, the gate maybe, might restore some spark of recognition. Even as he'd driven them through Redcliffe village he had been surprised when she'd shown no sign of remembering. And now — not even the house as the car pulled up outside.

She remained silent, a bewildered expression on her face as he led her up the steps and into the house. He helped her off with her coat and took her into the drawing room where he left her and went into the kitchen to make some tea.

When he returned with the tea she was settled on the window seat gazing out at the garden. As he set the tray down she spoke. 'I feel as if I'm in the middle of a desert and don't know how I got here, where I've been, or where I'm heading. A shutter has been pulled down on my life. I see nothing behind me but empty space — and nothing ahead. You tell me that you know very little about me Charlie except that I came here to visit my aunt and that as far as you know she was my only living relative. Which means that I'm alone in the world. I belong nowhere at present. It's quite frightening.'

He saw tears in her eyes and said gently, 'I think that you belong here at Grandstone House. You said you would love to stay here and never return to New York. You've left nothing behind there, no property, or apartment lease. You settled all that before you came. I know that you never intended to go back.'

She remained silent as she sipped her tea.

While Charlie drank his he mused . . . I might have at one time thought of marriage with this girl — for reasons no longer important; not for love. But for the present she needed his help and support. He must take on the responsibility for her. 'I shall stay for a while until you are completely settled in

349

here. I've asked the family lawyer to call and arrange the transfer of the deeds of the house over to you.'

She was about to protest but he held up his hand to silence her. 'This is the way I want things. This is the way it will be. I have also arranged for a woman to come and live in to help with the running of the house for the present. If she's not to your liking you can engage someone else of your own choice. I have explained that to her. I've made a list of domestic agencies and left it on the desk in the library. But I think you will be happy with her. She's a widow and a stranger to Redcliffe. She's been in this week helping to prepare the house for your return. At present she's renting a room in town — not the village. She will arrive here tomorrow to settle in if you like the look of her. I believe you will.'

He had especially gone to a domestic agency in town to engage a woman who was not a local resident and therefore not equipped to mention the past. 'I have also employed a gardener, very quiet, retired, lives alone and doesn't mind hard work.' To achieve this he had gone to the best source of local information — the village post office. More precisely the postmistress. Village post offices are always the best information bureaux on local lives. He had not been disappointed. She was an understanding soul and knew of a man who would not gossip, or even refer to the recent crimes that had been committed at Grandstone House. 'George Bailey, an old bachelor, never says a word to anyone except to pass the time o'day,' she had informed Charlie. 'Likes to be always on the go. Keeps his own cottage and garden as tidy as can be. Always been the same. Lived in the village for years. Always lived alone too. He seems to like to keep himself busy. I'm sure he'd be only too willing to take on the work. Lives in Field Lane — number six.'

For the very reason of the man's laconism Charlie had considered him ideal for the job. He seemed very keen and had professed a willingness to work all the hours required rather than they take on an extra pair of hands to begin with. Charlie had suggested this might be necessary to catch up on the neglect that had been inevitable while he was involved with so much else.

He had already shown him over the estate and briefed him on what was required to maintain the grounds in good order. George Bailey had already started work on the gardens. Charlie had worked with him for a few days to ease the workload.

Although he knew that the village people

would not openly question Sally Lane about the shocking events that had occurred at Grandstone House, or about her accident in the lane, much speculation about her would be inevitable. Whenever she went into the village she would for a while be the focus of mute attention. Never would she be accepted on familiar terms with the local people. To these she would always remain a foreigner who now lived in a once respectable house where shootings and murder had coincided with her visit. No such drama had occurred before in the quiet village of Redcliffe. At the same time she would be treated with the deference that is always a natural response towards the materially endowed. Eventually curiosity, frustrated by time, would fade and die.

They had both been silent for a while, staring out at the garden. Charlie wondered what was passing through her clouded mind at present. He rose from the window seat and went across to poke the logs into brighter flames in the firegrate. Then he seated himself in the wing-back.

After a moment or two she got up and seated herself in an armchair opposite him. She leaned towards the fire and rubbed her hands together as though cold. Then she spoke. 'Charlie — you must allow me to buy

352

the house from you. I can't allow you to just give it to me. You tell me that it was left to you in the will by my aunt. It seems so strange speaking about someone whom I don't recollect at all. She must have wanted you to have it. Surely you must want it — it's beautiful and . . . '

Shaking his head he interrupted. 'This house holds memories for me which I want to forget. Memories can't be sold.'

'But it's your home — where will you . . . ?'

'I've made plans. Don't concern yourself about me.'

'But . . . '

'No buts,' he cut in. 'You've said all your buts. It will be as I've arranged. Your name will be on the deeds of Grandstone House.' He paused briefly and repeated, 'Your name.'

'My name Charlie!' She gave a restricted half laugh. 'I don't even know that. So it's as well you do.'

24

Seated at his desk in Whitehall Clive Wessley gazed into space with eyes that bore the receipt of many sleepless nights. He had refused to take the leave offered by his chief. He would not be spending his weekends at home in Redcliffe for a long while yet. Work would be his only salvation from the torturing thoughts of self-reproach and reprimand which at present dominated his mind. He considered that he had handled the dangerous situation wrongly and badly that fateful night in Grandstone House. He should have ordered Charlie to remain outside the bedroom. Instead they had both rushed in after hearing Lydie scream. Personal feelings had prevailed over experience and training. At the same time they hadn't been aware that the American maniac was in the house and in possession of a gun. Nothing outside had betrayed his presence. They hadn't found the car until much later. He might well have surrendered the gun if he'd thought reinforcements were outside the room to cut off his escape . . . and Lydie might not have been . . . He groaned in tune with the wretched thoughts that had run through his mind unceasingly since her death. 'Oh God,' he moaned. It was all futile speculation now: Hindsight on what might or might not have happened if he had acted differently, all negative and unproductive. It had happened and nothing on earth could undo it. Yet he just couldn't stop this mental thrashing. He knew too that he'd been negligent in placing the revolver on the table in the upper corridor outside the bedroom. Even more so in placing the wheelchair within its reach, despite having thought that Emily was disabled and harmless.

At the same time he had wanted to put the gun out of the reach of his own itching fingers hell-bent on vengeance. Through his careless action he had made a criminal of an old lady and brought about the final stroke that killed her.

Earlier Charlie had phoned to explain about his having relinquished the title deeds of Grandstone House and to say that he would soon be leaving for good.

He had to admit that at first he had been a little sceptical with regards Charlie's real motive in taking on the gardening position; at least he had been until he'd met Lydie. But now — with this proposed walking away from it all — it proved beyond those earlier doubts that gain was of no interest to him. Charlie had asked him to keep an eye on the girl's welfare when he was gone himself, and asked if he would call in on her whenever he spent the weekends at home. Well he would do that for sure when the time came. Although he had explained that it wouldn't be for a while yet. In the meantime he would keep in contact with her by telephone in case she needed his help or advice. He could appreciate a little of how she must be feeling at present; a stranger to herself and her surroundings as well as to the people about her. His mother had promised to drop in at Grandstone House regularly to keep an eye on her. He knew that she would take the girl completely under her wing and make herself responsible for her until she had recovered her health, and even possibly her memory: until when many unanswered questions would remain.

He wasn't completely satisfied that Martha Oakes had told him all she knew. But no doubt time would tell. Hopefully the obscured past would not remain dormant in the girl's memory indefinitely.

He knew nothing of the last transcribed messages written on the pad by Lydie, or the revelations in the diary and the returned letter. Nor would he *ever know* from the lips of Charlie.

He didn't blame Charlie for wanting to leave the house, still so fresh from the scene of Lydie's death. Try as he might he couldn't banish it from his own mind and knew that it would remain in his memory forever, along with the sight of Charlie as he knelt to cradle her in his arms as she died. Always he would hear their last words to each other, and wonder what kind of love it was that had surfaced in those final moments?

Had it been merely the love of a very close and life-long friendship?

25

'Why won't you at least keep the car Charlie? I can't even drive.'

Resolute he shook his head as he replied, 'You can always learn.'

He wanted to take nothing from Grandstone House. Dressed in his tweed top-coat against the cold February wind he was on the brink of departure, his two suitcases at his feet on the marble floor. He had done all that he felt he possibly could to see that everything was settled with regards to the running of the household and the estate. The housekeeper whom he had chosen had been readily approved of by Sally Lane and had already settled into Martha Oakes's old room.

But before he left there was still some thing very important he must say. The time had come to say it. He had especially left it until this final moment. 'I have to ask you to promise me something. It's very important.'

'Anything Charlie. You've been so kind to me.'

'I want you to promise me that you'll contact me when you regain your memory, and I feel certain you will in time. Call me immediately, whatever the time, wherever you are. I shall come. Will you remember that. Promise me?'

'Of course I will Charlie. I promise most faithfully.' She studied his earnest face. 'I feel as though you know more about me than you've told me.'

He saw that her eyes had filled with tears again and for the moment took her hand in his. 'Believe me — there's nothing I can tell you that would help you in any way at all.'

Satisfied she nodded and clung to his hand for a moment longer. 'Will you come back some time to collect your papers from the top drawer of the desk in the library? The ones you said you were leaving there for the time being.'

'One day perhaps. For now I want you to leave the drawer as it is. I've locked it and have the key with me. There's not another in the house. I'll come back only if you contact me to say that you've remembered. Now please trust me.'

'I hope I do call you back very soon Charlie. I do so hope that. Don't forget to send me your address and telephone number so that I can at least contact you sometimes. I shall feel completely cut off otherwise.'

'I shan't forget. The minute I get settled in somewhere I'll let you know.'

A knock came on the front door and he

picked up his cases and went out to the waiting taxi.

He turned to give a last wave to her as he was driven away from the life that in the end had cost him so dearly.

* * *

Eyes lingered on him with passing interest as he walked along the busy London Street, plunged into an abyss of grief in a world that for him had stopped.

Under the TOFF DOMESTIC AGENCY sign he paused to glance up. He was recalling the day when he had walked out of its elegant doors buoyant with the hope of unknown but promising prospects ahead. Promising! Promising what? The death of Lydie.

Again he envied Sally Lane the oblivion of a forgotten past.

He walked on. Ten minutes later he stopped outside the entrance of a large hotel. By his own merit he would earn an existence. Diligence would engage his mind to some degree of forgetfulness. If this hotel had no need of his services then he would try another. London was full of hotels.

He set his shoulders and entered the great swing doors with his same old confidence.

But . . . he was not the same old Charlie.